DISNEY

THE
Magic
Kitchen
COOKBOOK

Meredith, Books
Des Moines, IA

Meredith Books
1716 Locust Street
Des Moines, IA 50309-3023
meredithbooks.com

Printed in China.

First Edition.
Library of Congress Control Number: 2007931157
ISBN: 978-0-696-23732-4

Senior Editor: Stephanie Karpinske, R.D.
Editor: Sheena Chihak, R.D.
Art Direction: Doug Samuelson, Chad Jewell
Graphic Design and Support Illustration: Mada Design, Inc.

Contents

Hello, all you young chefs and culinary experts out there! What? You don't consider yourself a culinary expert? Well, you soon will be with the help of this cookbook. First read through this section, where you'll learn a bit about food and how to prepare it. You'll also get a quick lesson in nutrition from Kim Possible and some activity tips from Dash, your friend from the Incredible family. After that, you'll be ready to get cooking. Flip through the book and you'll find recipes plus tons of food facts and information that will turn any humdrum meal into a dynamic dining experience!

So what are you waiting for? Let's get cooking!

STOP! ALERT!

ERR! Wait a minute! This is very important. Cooking is creative and fun, but sometimes cooking can also be slightly dangerous. Stoves are **HOT!** Knives are **SHARP!** Spilling boiling liquids can **HURT!**

So, before you show your culinary expertise in the kitchen, talk to the grown-ups in your home. Make sure they know what you're doing. Ask them for help if you're not sure about **ANYTHING.** Many of these dishes you can cook on your own, but you may need help from an adult on some. So don't hesitate—get a grown-up!

Whew! Okay, now we can move on!

Before you begin cooking, read this list. In fact, copy it and use it as a checklist! Then there will be no mistake about what you should do.

Before You Begin

☐ The first step in any cooking endeavor is to **READ!** Otherwise, how will you know what to cook, right? **READ** the entire **RECIPE** from start to finish. Ask yourself: Do I understand exactly what I'm supposed to do? If not, ask an adult for help.

☐ The next step is an **INGREDIENTS CHECK.** Check to see that you have all the ingredients you need, and that you have enough of each ingredient too. If you don't, make a list of the things you need and ask an adult to help you buy them.

☐ **GATHER** all the **EQUIPMENT.** Will you need mixing bowls and mixers? Get them out! Will you need measuring cups and baking pans? Get them out! Make sure they're clean and ready to use.

While You're Cooking

☐ Don't skip steps! Finish each step in the recipe before starting the next one. Otherwise, you could miss something really important, and then your dish might not be quite as tasty. And you don't want people making weird faces when they eat what you've cooked, right?

☐ Measure ingredients accurately!

☐ **STOP! ALERT!**
Use good food-safety habits!

When You're Done

☐ Cooking can be **MESSY!** That's what makes it so much fun! Leaving a mess behind, though, is not fun. So clean up after you cook. Clean any **EQUIPMENT** and put it away.

☐ Load **DIRTY DISHES** in the dishwasher or wash and dry them.

☐ Wipe **COUNTERS** with hot, soapy water.

☐ Wipe the **TABLE** clean too.

☐ Put away any **FOOD** that can be saved, like flour and butter.

☐ Throw away any **TRASH**, like food wrappers, empty packages, and eggshells.

☐ If the trash is overflowing or smelly, take it out! Show your family that you not only cook well, but that you clean up great too.

Measuring Matters!

Ah, the magic of cooking! A recipe is like a magic formula. If you follow it correctly, you'll end up with something simply delicious. If you make a mistake, however—hoo, boy!

That's why measuring is so important. So here are some tips for how to properly measure ingredients.

Measuring Liquids
This is done best with a measuring cup. The measuring cup should be made of clear glass or plastic. See the lines on the cup? These lines show you amounts. Set the cup on a flat surface, then pour in the liquid. Bend down so your eyes are level with the measurement marks. Do you need more or less? Add more or pour some out. If the amount you need is really small, like a teaspoon or a tablespoon, then get out your measuring spoons.

Measuring Dry Ingredients
Dry ingredients are things like flour, sugar, and shredded cheese. For these, use metal or plastic measuring cups and spoons. Metal or plastic measuring cups come in sets, and each cup is sized for a different amount. Choose the cup size the recipe calls for and spoon the ingredient into it. Move the flat edge of a table knife across the top to make it level with the cup. Use the measuring spoons for smaller amounts in the same way.

But What If . . .
. . . you don't have a measuring cup or spoon that's the right size? Easy! Just choose a smaller size and add them up to the amount you need. For example, if you don't have a $2/3$ cup, then measure $1/3$ cup—twice!

Watch Out!
Don't measure ingredients directly over the bowl or pan that all your ingredients go into. Why, you ask? Well, what if while you're measuring you spill stuff into the bowl with everything else? Errr! Not good! You'll have to start over. So measure your ingredients over a sink or a paper towel for easy cleanup in case you do spill.

Kitchen Basics!

It's time to get a tour of the kitchen to see where all the magic happens. Let's begin by learning how to understand a recipe. Sometimes when you're cooking, you come across words in recipes that make absolutely no sense. It's like you're reading a foreign language! But it's not. So hang on! Here we go!

BAKE. To cook food in an oven. (You probably knew that one!)

BEAT. To mix really, really well. When you beat something, you add air to it and make it smooth. You can beat something with a hand mixer or an electric mixer. You can also beat the food with a fork or a wooden spoon.

BOIL. To cook food on top of a stove over high heat. When something boils, you'll see lots of big bubbles pop on the surface.

STOP! ALERT! Boiling liquids are HOT! And hot things can BURN! Don't touch a pot of boiling liquid without a hot pad. Or better yet, ask a grown-up to do it. DON'T GET BURNED!

CHILL. To put food in a refrigerator until it is completely cold. BRRR!

CHOP. To cut food into small, pea-size pieces. When you chop, you'll need a knife and a cutting board. First cut the food into small, even slices. Then cut the slices into smaller, pea-size pieces. You can also chop foods with an electric blender or a food processor.

STOP! ALERT! Knives are SHARP! If you don't use them properly, you might cut yourself. OUCH! Have an adult show you the best way to hold and use a knife. Also have an adult watch you to make sure you chop correctly. Or better yet, let a grown-up do it. DON'T GET CUT!

COMBINE. To mix ingredients together. Just stir them all up. No need to beat them here.

COOL. To let food stand until it is no longer hot. You can set the food on the counter on top of a hot pad or — even better — use a wire cooling rack! Food will cool more evenly and quickly if it sits on a wire cooling rack because air can move around it.

COVER. To put plastic wrap, foil, or waxed paper over food to keep the air out. Keeping out the air prevents food from spoiling.

DASH. A dash is less than $1/8$ of a teaspoon. To add a dash, sprinkle a little into your palm. Then add it to what you are cooking.

DRAIN. To put food in a colander or a sieve so liquid pours out and solids are left behind. You might do this when you're cooking spaghetti or washing vegetables.

GREASE/LIGHTLY COAT. To put a light covering of butter, margarine, or nonstick cooking spray on a pan. Greasing keeps the food from sticking. Sticking can cause even the greatest culinary creation to become a culinary disaster!

MEASURE. To use a specific amount of an ingredient. (See "Measuring Matters," page 5).

MIX. To stir ingredients together so a mixture looks the same all over. Mixing is more than combining but not as much as beating.

PEEL. To remove the outer skin of vegetables or fruits. If the skin is thin, like on apples or potatoes, the best way to peel is with a peeler. If the skin is thick, like on bananas or oranges, you can peel the skin away with your fingers.

SIMMER. To cook food on top of a stove over high heat until lots of small bubbles come to the surface and break gently. Once the bubbles appear, turn the heat to low. Sometimes you might have to cover your simmering food too. Check the recipe first.

SLICE. To cut food into thin, even pieces. When you slice, you'll need a knife and a cutting board. Hold the food firmly on the board, then cut a thin piece off the end. Repeat, cutting until you have all the slices you need.

WHISK. To beat ingredients together using a whisk. When you whisk, you add air to the mixture. This makes the mixture light and fluffy.

In the Kitchen

Now that you've learned some culinary lingo, let's review the cooking tools you'll need as you make the recipes in this book. Find out how much you know about the kitchen! Try to identify all the cooking tools you see here. For each tool, write the letter from the list. Check your answers at the bottom of the page.

A. measuring cup

B. cutting board

C. whisk

D. electric mixer

E. frying pan

F. wooden spoon

G. measuring spoons

H. large pot

I. colander

J. tongs

K. spatula

L. peeler

1.____

2.____

3.____

4.____

5.____

6.____

7.____

8.____

9.____

10.____

11.____

12.____

COOKING SMART= COOKING SAFE!

The kitchen is one place where you need to follow some simple, but very important, safety rules. So read this section at least once, maybe twice!

FOOD RULES!

Did you know that if you don't take care of your food, it can make you sick? You don't want foul food in your kitchen fouling up your recipes. Blech! Food will be tasty and safe to eat if you keep everything clean! That means your hands, the food, the equipment, and all work surfaces—everything! Keeping everything clean doesn't give bacteria a chance to land and spread their foulness. So follow these simple food rules to help you properly handle and store food:

• Wash fresh fruits and vegetables in cool water before eating or preparing them.

• Don't use cracked or dirty eggs! They may be contaminated with harmful bacteria. After working with eggs, always wash your hands, your equipment, and the countertop.

• Don't eat raw eggs! Those harmful bacteria might be hanging out here too. Cooking the eggs will kill the bacteria. So no raw eggs for you!

• Don't eat raw meat! Like raw eggs, fish, poultry (chicken, turkey), and beef must be well cooked to kill harmful bacteria. Make sure your meats are cooked all the way through!

• Put away leftovers as soon as possible! Put leftovers into covered containers and refrigerate or freeze them as soon as possible. Leftovers should not sit out for more than 2 hours after cooking. Otherwise, guess what? Those icky bacteria will be happy to make a home there.

• Keep cold foods cold! Foods you put in the refrigerator, like deli meat and cheese, should be cold when you touch them. Frozen foods should be icy and firm. Once you're finished with them, wrap them back up and put them away. Keep them cold! Also, it isn't safe to thaw foods on the countertop. Thaw them overnight in the refrigerator instead. (You can also thaw foods in the microwave IF you are going to cook them right away.)

And don't forget:

Wash your hands with lots of soap and water for at least 20 seconds before you start to cook!

Whew! That's a lot to remember, but most of it is common sense. Still, if you're not sure about anything, read these pages again.

And what else? ASK AN ADULT!

Got Questions?

Get help! Sure, you can probably do a lot of the cooking on your own. But adults **LOVE** feeling useful. Read the recipe with a grown-up, then ask any questions. For example:

• Not sure which equipment and ingredients you need?
  Have no fear! A grown-up is here!

• Not sure which equipment is safe to use on your own?
  When in doubt, give a grown-up a shout!

• Not sure how to use the equipment?
  Don't get all bothered! Give a grown-up a holler!

Dress the Part!

If you want to be a chef, then you have to dress the part. So start by putting on an apron. Aprons protect your clothes from spills and splatters. You'll also want to roll up your sleeves. Oh, and tie back your hair! That keeps your food—and yourself—safe.

Don't Get Burned!

Anything you take from the oven, microwave, or stove will be **HOT! Yee-oow!** So to protect your hands, always use hot pads or oven mitts. To protect counters and other surfaces, always place a hot pan or a hot pot on a hot pad or a cooling rack.

Don't Get Steamed!

Here's another tip. Ready? Steam is hot and can burn! So don't get steamed—get smart! Before you lift the lid from a hot pot, release a bit of steam first. Open the lid slightly on the side farthest from you.

Avoid the Bump!

Bumping the handle of a pot or pan while it's on the stove can make a big, hot mess. **Agh!** To avoid messy mishaps, turn pot and pan handles to the middle of the stove.

Turn Us Off!

You want to get all the stuff out of your mixing bowl, but the bowl is attached to a mixer or a blender, so turn it off! Unplug it too! Also unplug before you put in or take out the beaters.

Water Warning!

Electric appliances and water do not mix! Do not use an electric appliance near water. If an appliance accidentally falls into water while it's plugged in, **DON'T TOUCH IT!** Call a grown-up for help. Never plug in or unplug appliances when your hands are wet.

We Don't Belong!

Not everything in the kitchen can be used in the microwave oven. Aluminum foil, foil containers, metal pans, silverware, and some glass or pottery dishes can cause sparks. Yikes! Make sure the things you put in the microwave are microwave safe.

Handle Us With Care!

This is **REALLY** important! So **LISTEN CLOSELY!** Because . . .**KNIVES ARE SHARP!!** Sometimes you need sharp utensils for cooking. What you don't need is to cut yourself! Here are some ways to make sure you remain bandage free:

• **Handle First!** Always pick up a knife or kitchen scissors by the handle.

• **Keep Them in Sight!** Leave all sharp items on the counter until you are ready to wash them. If you put them in a sink full of soapy water, you might not see them. You might reach in and—OUCH!—accidentally cut yourself.

• **Point Away!** Always keep the sharp edge of a knife pointed away from you and your hand when cutting food.

In Case of Emergency

Sometimes accidents do happen. That's why it is important to know where the first-aid kit is. If you burn yourself or touch something hot, hold your hand under cold water right away. Aaaahhh!

The Supermarket—A Chef's Paradise!

Ah! To stroll through a supermarket, with row after row of fine, fresh food! Why, it is a chef's paradise! Here you can choose the best foods to make incredibly delectable dishes.

Before you go to the grocery store, it is best to have a plan. Preparing a scrumptious meal takes planning. And so does going to the grocery store. So, here's the plan:

1. Read your recipe.
2. Write down each ingredient you need and how much.
3. Look through your kitchen for the ingredients on your list.
4. If you have enough of an ingredient, then cross it off.
5. If you don't have enough, then circle it.

NOW, LET'S GO SHOPPING!

THE Dairy AISLE

The first thing you'll notice when you go to the store is that many foods that have something in common are all found in the same place. For example, suppose your recipe calls for butter, milk, and cheese. These foods are all dairy foods. And guess what else? All these foods are found in the dairy section of the store! Want to know something else about dairy foods? Dairy foods are good for you! They have calcium, which keeps your bones and teeth strong and healthy.

Breads AND Grains

Mmmmmmmm! Aaaaaaah! Do you smell that? That's bread, freshly baked and out of the oven. You can find lots of different breads in the bread or bakery aisle. Bread is part of the grain family because it's made of wheat, and wheat is a grain. Pasta is also a grain, and so is rice. Foods made from grains have carbohydrates, which give your body energy.

Note to Parents:

The recipes in this book suggest using white whole wheat flour. There is a reason for that. White whole wheat flour is a good way to get your whole grains. It is healthier for you than all-purpose flour. You can gradually change your family's diet to include white whole wheat flour by mixing in a little bit with the all-purpose flour, like this: If a recipe calls for a cup of flour, use $1/3$ cup of white whole wheat and $2/3$ cup of all-purpose. See if your family notices a difference. The next time you cook, use more white whole wheat flour, and so on. You'll find that your foods won't taste all that different, yet they'll be much richer in vitamins, minerals, and fiber.

THE Meat AISLE

Do you want strong muscles? Well, they don't just grow overnight. You have to keep your muscles active and eat foods with protein and iron. And one of the best sources of protein and iron is meat, such as chicken, steaks, ground beef, turkey, and ham. Nuts and beans also have protein and iron, but they are found in the middle of the store (check the store signs for where to find them).

Fruits AND Vegetables

Looking for apples, oranges, bananas, grapes, peppers, onions, or cucumbers? You've come to the right place. It's the produce section, where you'll find lots of fresh fruits and vegetables. Fruits and vegetables add color and flavor to your cooking. Plus, they are full of vitamins and minerals that your body needs to stay healthy. You should eat lots of them each day!

Frozen Foods

If you see a bunch of food behind glass and feel a chill in the air, you're probably in the frozen foods aisle. You can find all sorts of good foods here, like frozen fruits and vegetables. Even frozen grains, like whole wheat waffles and breads, are just a door away!

Oh my! It's easy to get overwhelmed at the supermarket. But just remember to make a list of everything you need before you go. Then stick to the plan!

POWER UP WITH THE ...
POWER PLATE!

Hey, guys! So tell me—what's the sitch with food? Like, how do you know how much to eat of one thing over another? It can be so totally confusing, right?

Well, that's why I'm here! I, Kim Possible, am going to show you how easy it is to eat right. And I should know. After all, when your mom is a surgeon and your dad is a rocket scientist, who do you think gets stuck planning meals? It's not like I don't have anything else to do, right?

That's why I choose to simplify and make eating right so not the drama. And that's where this handy little device comes in. It's what I call—are you ready?

MY POWER PLATE! Pretty cool, huh?

FRUITS — — DAIRY
MEAT, FISH, — — GRAINS
BEANS, NUTS — — VEGETABLES

The Power Plate shows you which food groups you're eating from at each meal so you know which food groups you need to add to the meal.

Oh—what's a food group? A food group is a bunch of foods that are all alike. For example, apples and oranges and bananas are all fruits. They all belong to the Fruit Group. Milk, cheese, and yogurt are all dairy foods. They belong to the Dairy Group. Chicken, beef, and fish are types of meats. They all belong to the Meat Group. (Pretty easy, right? You don't need to be a rocket scientist to figure that out!)

Foods that are grouped together also tend to have similar nutrients in them. (We'll talk more about nutrients later.) That's why you'll find nuts and beans mixed in with the meat group. These foods, like meat, have a lot of iron and protein, which are nutrients.

I know what your next question is:

But how much, EXACTLY, am I supposed to eat of each food?! The answer to that question actually differs from person to person. Some people need more servings of a food group than others. It has to do with your age and whether you're a boy or a girl. Look at this chart, then find your age and your gender. Run your finger along the row to see how much of each food you should eat.

	Grains	Vegetables	Fruits	Dairy	Meats, etc.
Boys and girls, 4–8 years old	4–5 ounces a day	1½ cups a day	1½ cups a day	1–2 cups a day	3–4 ounces a day
Girls, 9–13 years old	5 ounces a day	2 cups a day	1½ cups a day	3 cups a day	5 ounces a day
Boys, 9–13 years old	6 ounces a day	2½ cups a day	1½ cups a day	3 cups a day	5 ounces a day

So now you're wondering:

What makes up an ounce or a cup? Do I have to measure every food I eat? Yikes! No way! It's not as dramatic as all that. Here are some common foods to help you figure out a 1-ounce or a 1-cup serving.

Grains	Vegetables	Fruits	Dairy	Meats, etc.
A 1-ounce serving equals:	**A cup is . . .**	**A cup is . . .**	**A cup is . . .**	**A 1-ounce serving equals:**
• a slice of bread	• 3 spears of broccoli	• a small apple	• 1 container of yogurt (8 ounces)	• 1 ounce beef, poultry, or fish
• ½ cup of oatmeal	• 2 medium carrots	• a large banana	• 1 cup milk	• 1 egg
• 1 cup of cold cereal	• a large ear of corn on the cob	• a medium grapefruit	• 2 slices or 1½ ounces of cheese	• 1 tablespoon of peanut butter
• ½ cup of rice or pasta	• 1 whole tomato	• 32 grapes	• 1½ cups ice cream	• a handful of nuts
	• 2 stalks of celery	• a large orange	• 1 cup frozen yogurt	• ¼ cup of dried beans
		• a large peach		

And your next question is:

Why is it important that I eat more of one food than another? Good question! The answer is because different foods have different nutrients. Nutrients are the elements in foods that make them good—or bad—for us. Here are the major nutrients, how they help us, and where you'll find them:

Major Nutrient	Why We Need It	Where We Find It
PROTEIN	Protein strengthens the tissues in your body. That might not seem like a big job, but it is. Why? Because your body's muscles, organs (like your heart), and immune system are made of tissues! So if you eat plenty of protein, you'll keep these things strong and healthy.	**Dairy Foods, Meats, Fish, Poultry, and Nuts**
CARBOHYDRATES	Your body changes carbohydrates into sugar, and then uses the sugar for energy. When you exercise, you burn these sugars. BUT if you eat too many carbohydrates and don't exercise enough, your body stores the sugars. The sugars build up and then you gain weight. That's why eating and exercising go hand in hand.	**Grains and Fruits**
VITAMINS AND MINERALS	Vitamins and minerals keep your body running like a well-oiled machine. Each vitamin and mineral helps your body in a different way. Some keep your bones strong, like calcium. Others fight off germs, like vitamin C. If you eat a balanced diet, you'll get all the vitamins and minerals your body needs.	**All the Food Groups have some: Fruits and Vegetables are full of them**
FATS	Although you shouldn't eat too many foods that have fats, fats do play an important role. Your body does need some fats. Fats absorb vitamins, helping your body process them. Fats also give you some energy.	**Meat and Dairy Foods**

I know, I know! That's a lot to digest. (Sorry! I couldn't resist!) Eating a healthy, balanced diet is not hard work. It's a matter of choosing the right foods and eating plenty of them, and not eating too many foods that aren't good for you. Follow the Power Plate, and you'll be on your way to a healthier, more powerful you!

ENERGIZE AND EXERCISE!

Yahoo! Before you get cooking, I need to tell you one more thing. You've learned a ton of stuff about food so far. But your body also needs something else. And that is . . . **EXERCISE!!** Take it from me, Dash. Running at top speeds is FUN! It just feels GOOD! Your legs are pumping, your arms are moving, the wind is breezing through your hair. Yahoo! I LOVE it! Exercising and being active is so cool!

Check It Out!

Look at all the ways that being active helps your body:
- It makes your muscles and your bones strong.
- It keeps your body fat in check, which means you'll maintain a healthy weight.
- It helps your body fight diseases.
- It helps you sleep better.
- It makes you feel great throughout the day.

With so many things going for it, how can you not exercise?

So here are some awesome activities you can try to keep your body in top shape. The activities can be grouped according to the three secret ingredients of physical fitness: endurance, strength, and flexibility. Ready? Here we go!

Pump It Up—Endurance!

Endurance means how long something can last. When you do activities to build up your endurance, you're making your heart pump really fast. You can probably feel it jumping around in your chest. You breathe a lot quicker too. That's because your body is using a lot of oxygen. Your blood is zooming around your body, delivering oxygen all over, like to your muscles. These activities will help you build up your endurance:

- **RUNNING! Yahoo! See if you can run as fast as me!**
- **Dancing! Put on your favorite tunes and dance to some fast songs.**
- **Bicycling! Strap on your helmet, hop on your bike, and get pedaling.**
- **Run around and shoot some hoops!**
- **Run around with a soccer ball and score some goals!**
- **In-line skating! Put on your protective gear and get going.**
- **Play a game of tag with your friends! Run around and try not to get tagged!**
- **If it's snowing—try to run through the snow!**

 Safety Alert: Always walk through your neighborhood with an adult. And only talk to your neighbors if you know them. When you exercise with your friends, play fair. Don't knock each other down or push kids out of the way. Exercising means having fun, not getting hurt.

Build It Up—Strength!

When you think about someone who is really strong (like my dad, Mr. Incredible), you think of someone with tons of muscles. The more you use your muscles, the stronger they get. You can strengthen your muscles with these activities:

- **Climb a tree or a jungle gym!** Climbing strengthens your arm and leg muscles.
- **Run uphill!** This strengthens your leg muscles.
- **Do push-ups!** They're great for your arm and chest muscles.
- **Do sit-ups!** They're great for your stomach muscles.
- **Go hiking with your family!** When you hike, your leg muscles get a workout.
- **If it's snowing, build a snowman!** Rolling big balls of snow builds up arm strength.

 Safety Alert: Whenever you leave your home, tell a grown-up where you're going. Make sure you have permission and that it is safe. Have an adult check your bike, helmet, in-line skates, or other sports equipment to make sure it's safe before you use it.

Stretch It Out—Flexibility!

My mom, Elastigirl, is an ace at stretching. Your body will have a hard time doing much of anything if it's stiff and can't bend. When you're flexible, your arms and legs move easily and your body can bend. To keep your body flexible, add some of these moves into your other activities:

- **If you're dancing, add some body twists and deep knee bends.**
- **If you're playing basketball, twist and bend at the waist.**
- **Try somersaults or the splits to keep your body flexible.**
- **Try to reach up toward the sky, stretching your body as far as it will go.**

Do you know what the hardest part of being physically fit is? The hardest part of exercising and being active is . . .
Turning off the TV or the computer! That's right! Exercising is the easy part. Getting out there and doing it—that's the hard part. But it's as easy as pushing the off button. Get out and exercise about an hour a day, and—yahoo!—you'll be feeling like you can beat me in any race, any time. And maybe I'll let you win! (Nah, I doubt it!)

Check It Out!

Don't forget to drink water! When you exercise, your body sweats and loses water. So drink plenty of water—even when you're not exercising. It's a great way to keep your body hydrated and healthy.

GET ACTIVE!

Throughout the book, look for this box for more fun ideas for staying active!

Go for a really fast walk and time yourself.

Incredible BREAK FASTS

Good morning! Looks like you're ready for school. Think you're ready to head out the door? Errr! Not so fast! You haven't eaten a nutritious and balanced breakfast!

Do you think the Incredibles skip their morning meal? Of course not! Each morning, Helen Parr (also known as "Elastigirl"—or "Mom") gets her clan ready for a day full of action. And boy, are they busy.

Dash loves to race, but he can't compete if he's not fully fueled. Violet needs a hearty breakfast to make it through a long day of high school. And Bob (also known as "Mr. Incredible"—or "Dad") can't save the world if he skips the first meal of the day.

So before you head out the door, recharge with a good breakfast.

JUNGLE FRENCH TOAST STICKS

INGREDIENTS

Nonstick cooking spray

1 small banana, peeled

6 slices whole grain or whole wheat bread

6 tablespoons tub-style light cream cheese

2 eggs

½ cup fat-free milk

⅛ teaspoon ground cinnamon (if you like)

Powdered sugar

UTENSILS

15×10×1-inch baking pan
cutting board
table knife
medium bowl
fork
measuring cups
measuring spoons
wide metal spatula
hot pads
wire cooling rack

1 Turn on the oven to 400°F. Lightly coat the baking pan with nonstick cooking spray. Save until Step 4. Put the banana on the cutting board. Use the table knife to slice the banana. If you like, cut the crust off each bread slice.

2 Spread the cream cheese on 3 of the bread slices. Top with banana slices. Put the other 3 bread slices on top. Put the sandwiches on the cutting board. Use the knife to cut each sandwich lengthwise into 3 pieces. Set pieces aside.

3 Crack the eggs into the medium bowl. Use the fork to beat the eggs until combined. Add the milk and cinnamon (if you like). Beat with the fork until mixed.

4 Dip a sandwich piece into the egg mixture, making sure to coat all sides. Hold it over the bowl to let the egg mixture drip off. Put in the prepared baking pan. Repeat with the remaining sandwich pieces and egg mixture. Pour any leftover egg mixture over sandwich pieces in pan.

5 Put the baking pan in the oven. Bake about 20 minutes or until pieces are brown and toasted, using the spatula to turn once halfway through baking time. Turn off oven. Use the hot pads to take the pan out of the oven. Put the pan on the wire rack.

6 Use the spatula to remove the French toast sticks. Serve warm sprinkled lightly with powdered sugar. Makes 9 sticks (2 or 3 sticks per serving).

Nutrition Facts per stick: 105 calories, 4 g total fat, 52 mg cholesterol, 132 mg sodium, 14 g carbohydrate, 4 g sugar, 3 g fiber, 6 g protein.

See how long you can jump rope without getting tangled. Use a timer to see how long you can go. Or just count how many times you can jump.

You'll go ape for these yummy breakfast sticks bursting with jungle-fresh bananas!

WAKE 'EM UP COWBOY BAGEL

INGREDIENTS

- **4 hard cooked eggs, peeled and cooled**
- **4 ounces thinly sliced cooked low-fat ham**
- **2 tablespoons light mayonnaise or salad dressing**
- **1 tablespoon yellow or Dijon-style mustard**
- **2 whole wheat bagels, 2 large whole wheat pita bread rounds, or four 6-inch whole wheat tortillas**

1 Put the eggs on the cutting board and use the sharp knife to cut the eggs into small pieces.

2 Put the chopped eggs into a bowl. Put the ham on the cutting board and use the sharp knife to cut the ham into small pieces. Add the ham, mayonnaise, and mustard to the chopped eggs in bowl. Use the wooden spoon to stir egg mixture until mixed.

3 Put the bagels on the cutting board and carefully use the sharp knife to cut each bagel in half. Top each bagel with $1/3$ cup of the egg mixture. (Or put pita bread rounds on the cutting board and use the sharp knife to cut each pita bread round in half crosswise. Using your fingers, carefully split open each half to form a pocket [be careful not to break into 2 pieces]. Spoon $1/3$ cup of the egg mixture into each pita pocket. Or spoon $1/3$ cup of the egg mixture near one edge of each tortilla and roll tortilla around egg mixture.) Makes 4 servings.

UTENSILS
- cutting board
- sharp knife
- bowls
- measuring spoons
- wooden spoon
- measuring cups

Nutrition Facts per serving: 259 calories, 10 g total fat, 230 mg cholesterol, 509 mg sodium, 25 g carbohydrate, 1 g sugar, 3 g fiber, 17 g protein.

Check This Out

More than 87,000,000,000 (that's 87 billion!) eggs are produced in America every year.

RISE AND SHINE, PARTNER! THIS EGG-FILLED BAGEL WILL HELP YOU WAKE UP AND BE READY FOR A BUSY MORNING.

IMPOSSIBLY EASY A.M. SUNDAES

INGREDIENTS

1 cup fresh blueberries, grapes, fresh strawberries, and/or 2 small bananas, peeled

1 6- to 8-ounce carton vanilla low-fat yogurt

½ to 1 cup ready-to-eat unsweetened cereal such as bran cereal flakes, round toasted oat cereal, and/or oat square cereal

UTENSILS

cutting board
sharp knife
small spoon
measuring cups
2 serving bowls

If you're hurrying to save the world or just short on time in the morning, try this so-simple sundae to get you going in no time.

1 If you are using strawberries, put them on the cutting board and use the sharp knife to cut off their green tops. Cut the strawberries into bite-size pieces. If you are using bananas, put them on the cutting board and use the knife to cut them into bite-size pieces.

2 Divide yogurt in half and spoon each half into a serving bowl. Divide cereal and fruit in half and put into bowls with yogurt. Serve right away. Makes 2 servings.

Nutrition Facts per serving: 151 calories, 1 g total fat, 4 mg cholesterol, 126 mg sodium, 32 g carbohydrate, 23 g sugar, 3 g fiber, 6 g protein.

Set up a cool obstacle course in your yard and have somebody time you going through it. Keep practicing and see if you can get a faster time!

Code Word: FRUIT

Unscramble the words in the story below.
Write them on the lines, then solve the secret code word.

I'm a good source of vitamin C and **(efibr)**. __ __ __ __ __

I help you fight **(easdise)** __ __ __ __ __ __ __
and remember things. Oh, and don't forget, I'll help you stay
(ouyng). __ __ __ __ __

I grow on **(ushbse)** __ __ __ __ __ __
during the **(ummsre)**. __ __ __ __ __ __

I'm **(ebul)** __ __ __ __ and sweet and good to eat.
I'm a kind of **(errby)**. __ __ __ __ __

Kim **(essbiPol)** __ __ __ __ __ __ __ __
says to eat lots of me to stay healthy.

What am I?

__ __ __ __ __ __ __ __ __

Unscramble the circled letters above
to find out what I am.

NOT TOO SCARY
BERRY PANCAKES

INGREDIENTS

- 1 cup white whole wheat or all-purpose flour
- 2 teaspoons sugar
- 2 teaspoons baking powder
- ¼ teaspoon salt
- 1 egg
- 1 cup fat-free milk
- 2 tablespoons canola oil
- 1 cup fresh or frozen blueberries
- ¼ cup chopped walnuts (if you like)
- Nonstick cooking spray
- ⅔ cup frozen light whipped dessert topping, thawed
- ½ cup vanilla low-fat yogurt

UTENSILS

- measuring cups
- measuring spoons
- 2 medium bowls
- wooden spoon
- fork
- griddle or large skillet
- pancake turner
- serving plate
- foil
- small bowl
- rubber scraper
- spoon

1 Put flour, sugar, baking powder, and salt in a medium bowl. Stir with wooden spoon to mix. Save until Step 3.

2 Crack the egg into the other medium bowl. Beat with the fork until the egg yolk and white are mixed. Add milk and oil to egg. Beat with the fork until ingredients are well mixed.

3 Add the egg mixture to the flour mixture. Stir with the wooden spoon until the mixture is wet and almost smooth. Gently stir in ½ cup of the blueberries and the walnuts (if you like).

4 Lightly coat the unheated griddle or large skillet with nonstick cooking spray. Put the griddle or skillet on the burner. Turn heat to medium and let griddle or skillet get hot. (To check if the griddle or skillet is ready, sprinkle a few drops of water on the surface. The water will dance across the surface when the griddle is hot enough.)

5 For each pancake, pour about ¼ cup of the batter onto the hot griddle or skillet. Cook over medium heat until pancakes have bubbly surfaces and the edges are dry. (This will take about 2 minutes.)

6 Turn the pancakes over with the pancake turner. Cook until bottoms are golden brown (about 2 minutes more). Remove pancakes from griddle or skillet and put on a serving plate. Cover with foil to keep warm. Repeat until all of the batter is used, stirring batter between batches of pancakes. Turn off burner. Remove griddle or skillet from burner.

7 Meanwhile, place dessert topping and yogurt in the small bowl. Stir with rubber scraper until mixed. Spoon yogurt mixture onto pancakes and sprinkle with the remaining ½ cup blueberries. Makes 8 servings.

Nutrition Facts per serving: 141 calories, 5 g total fat, 28 mg cholesterol, 195 mg sodium, 20 g carbohydrate, 8 g sugar, 2 g fiber, 5 g protein.

Check This Out
In New Jersey, blueberries are the official state fruit!

Scare away morning hunger with these berry-filled pancakes. After all, a balanced breakfast is no laughing matter!

As You Wish Muffins

INGREDIENTS

Nonstick cooking spray

1¾ cups white whole wheat flour

¼ cup sugar

2 teaspoons baking powder

¼ teaspoon salt

¼ teaspoon ground cinnamon

1 egg

¾ cup fat-free milk

¼ cup canola oil

¼ cup apricot, peach, or raspberry spreadable fruit

UTENSILS

12 paper bake cups

muffin pan with twelve 2½-inch cups

measuring cups

measuring spoons

2 medium bowls

wooden spoon

fork

spoons

hot pads

wire cooling rack

1 Heat the oven to 400°F. Put the paper bake cups in the muffin cups. Coat the insides of the paper cups lightly with nonstick cooking spray. Save until Step 3.

2 Put the flour, sugar, baking powder, salt, and cinnamon in a medium bowl. Stir with the wooden spoon to mix. Crack the egg into the other bowl. Add the milk and oil to the egg and beat with the fork until mixed.

3 Add the egg mixture to the flour mixture. Stir with the wooden spoon just until the mixture is wet. Spoon 1 tablespoon of the batter into each muffin cup. Spoon 1 teaspoon of the spreadable fruit on top of the batter in each cup. Spoon the remaining batter over the spreadable fruit.

4 Put the muffin pan in the oven. Bake for 15 to 18 minutes or until the tops of the muffins are lightly browned. Turn off oven. Use the hot pads to remove muffin pan from oven. Put the muffin pan on the wire rack and let cool for 10 minutes. Tip muffin pan to carefully remove muffins onto the wire rack. Serve warm. Makes 12 muffins.

Nutrition Facts per muffin: 140 calories, 5 g total fat, 18 mg cholesterol, 101 mg sodium, 22 g carbohydrate, 5 g sugar, 1 g fiber, 3 g protein.

Explore a whole new world when you lace up your hiking boots and hit the trails with your family!

OOH, I LIKE IT! MUY MUCHO! VERY NICE. YOUR WISH IS MY COMMAND!
YOU DON'T NEED A MAGIC GENIE TO GET THE BREAKFAST YOU'RE WISHING FOR. JUST FLAVOR THESE MUFFINS EXACTLY AS YOU WISH!

BOWL OF ENERGY BREAKFAST

*Jack-Jack is full of energy (just ask his babysitter!).
Use this apple oatmeal to fill yourself with energy
and you might find superpowers of your own!*

INGREDIENTS

1   **envelope plain instant oatmeal**

²/₃   **cup water**

¼   **cup unsweetened applesauce**

¼   **teaspoon apple pie spice**

UTENSILS

microwave-safe bowl
measuring cups
waxed paper
hot pads
wooden spoon
measuring spoons

1 Open oatmeal envelope. Pour oatmeal into a microwave-safe bowl. Add the water to the oatmeal. Cover with waxed paper. Put bowl in microwave oven and cook on 100% power (high) for 1 to 2 minutes or until thickened. Use hot pads to remove bowl from the microwave. Stir with a wooden spoon until mixed. Add applesauce and apple pie spice to oatmeal; stir until mixed. Makes 1 serving.

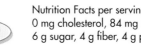 Nutrition Facts per serving: 131 calories, 2 g total fat, 0 mg cholesterol, 84 mg sodium, 25 g carbohydrate, 6 g sugar, 4 g fiber, 4 g protein.

 Oatmeal month is celebrated each January, when Americans buy more oatmeal than any other month of the year.

Tropical Fruit Smoothie

INGREDIENTS

- **1   medium banana, peeled**
- **1½   cups cut-up fresh fruit such as strawberries, raspberries, cantaloupe, honeydew melon, papaya, and/or kiwifruit**
- **1   6- to 8-ounce carton vanilla low-fat yogurt**
- **¾   cup fat-free milk**
- **Honey (if you like)**
- **Fresh fruit (if you like)**

UTENSILS

**cutting board
sharp knife
measuring cups
blender or food processor
rubber scraper
4 tall glasses**

1 Put the banana on the cutting board and use the sharp knife to cut it into chunks. Put the banana, cut-up fruit, yogurt, and milk in a blender or food processor. Cover and blend or process until mixture is smooth, scraping down sides with rubber scraper as needed. Pour into the tall glasses. If you like, stir in some honey and top with additional fresh fruit. Makes 4 servings.

Nutrition Facts per serving: 103 calories, 2 g total fat, 6 mg cholesterol, 48 mg sodium, 19 g carbohydrate, 26 g sugar, 2 g fiber, 4 g protein.

 **Americans eat more than 300,000 tons of yogurt each year.**

Start your morning luau-style! This tropical drink is a great way to get energized.

Don't Forget BREAKFAST COOKIES

INGREDIENTS

Nonstick cooking spray

$\frac{1}{2}$ cup butter, softened

$\frac{2}{3}$ cup packed brown sugar

1   teaspoon baking soda

2   eggs

$1\frac{3}{4}$ cups white whole wheat flour

3   cups multigrain cereal flakes
    with blueberries

UTENSILS

cookie sheet

measuring cups

large mixing bowl

electric mixer

measuring spoons

wooden spoon

rubber scraper

hot pads

wide metal spatula

wire cooling rack

1 Turn on the oven to 350°F. Coat the cookie sheet with nonstick cooking spray. Save until Step 3.

2 Put the butter in the mixing bowl. Beat with the electric mixer for 30 seconds. Add brown sugar and baking soda. Beat until mixed. Add the eggs; beat until mixed. Add flour and beat until the mixture no longer looks dry. Use the wooden spoon to stir in the cereal.

3 For each cookie, pack the mixture into a $\frac{1}{4}$-cup measuring cup. Use the rubber scraper to scrape it out of the cup onto the prepared cookie sheet. Press mound of dough with your fingers to flatten it slightly. Repeat with remaining dough, placing cookies about 3 inches apart.

4 Put the cookie sheet in the oven. Bake cookies for 8 to 10 minutes or until edges are golden brown. Turn off oven. Use hot pads to take the cookie sheet out of the oven. Let baked cookies stand on the cookie sheet for 1 minute. Use the wide spatula to transfer the cookies to the wire rack; let cookies cool. Makes 12 cookies.

Nutrition Facts per cookie: 227 calories, 9 g total fat, 56 mg cholesterol, 229 mg sodium, 34 g carbohydrate, 14 g sugar, 2 g fiber, 4 g protein.

Food Facts

Brown sugar is simply white sugar combined with molasses. The molasses makes the texture of brown sugar softer than white sugar.

No matter how forgetful you are in the morning, you're sure to remember breakfast when it comes as a cookie!

SCHOOL LUNCH

Woo-hoo! It's LUNCHTIME! Chicken Little LOVES lunchtime. He gets to hang out in the school cafeteria and meet up with his friends, like Runt, who likes to eat a bazillion ears of corn. Chicken Little's dad, Buck Cluck, packs his son a lunch that's full of foods that build up Chicken Little's muscles so maybe, someday, he can grow into a big baseball star like his dad.

Lunch is all about taking a break from work, school, and play. It's a time to get re-energized. These lunch recipes will not only do that, but they'll be sure to impress your friends too. Runt might even give up an ear of corn to swap for one of these delectable dishes.

Even if the sky is falling, remember these words that Chicken Little loves to belt out: "You're still a champion!"—if you have a great lunch.

SIGN UP FOR OAKEY OAKS LITTLE LEAGUE!

Foxy Loxy
Goosey Loosey
Abby Mallard
CHICKEN LITTLE

BAKE SALE SATURDAY!!

CLASS PHOTOS

LUNCH MENU

y Loxy makes

LIGHTNING-FAST WRAPS

INGREDIENTS

8 cherry tomatoes

2 10-inch tomato-basil, spinach, or whole grain flour tortillas*

¼ cup light toasted onion sour cream dip

4 very thin slices deli turkey, chicken, beef, or ham (about 4 ounces)

½ cup fresh spinach leaves

¼ cup purchased shredded carrot

1 Put the tomatoes on the cutting board. Use the sharp knife to halve each tomato.

2 Use the table knife to spread each tortilla with 2 tablespoons of the dip. Divide meat between tortillas. Top with spinach leaves, tomato, and carrot. Tightly roll up tortillas. Wrap tightly in plastic wrap. Chill in the refrigerator for up to 2 days. If desired, use a sharp knife to cut each wrap in half and then in half again so that you have four even pieces. Makes 2 to 4 servings.

Nutrition Facts per serving: 388 calories, 9 g total fat, 18 mg cholesterol, 939 mg sodium, 59 g carbohydrate, 6 g sugar, 6 g fiber, 16 g protein.

*Note: Fiber, protein, fat, and calories vary in these tortillas. Make sure to read labels and pick tortillas high in fiber and protein.

UTENSILS

cutting board
sharp knife
table knife
measuring cups
plastic wrap

Food Facts

The vitamin A in carrots can help you see in the dark!

WHETHER YOU'RE RACING IN THE PISTON CUP OR WORKING HARD AT SCHOOL, USE THESE SPEEDY WRAPS TO REFUEL YOUR BODY.

garden-fresh veggies salad

INGREDIENTS

¼ of a small cucumber

¼ cup grape or cherry tomatoes

1 ounce cooked turkey or ham

1 cup packaged torn mixed salad greens

2 tablespoons shredded mozzarella cheese

1 tablespoon sliced almonds or walnut pieces (if you like)

2 tablespoons of your favorite bottled reduced-fat or reduced-calorie salad dressing

UTENSILS

cutting board

sharp knife

measuring cups

4-cup plastic storage container with lid or 1-quart resealable plastic bag

small resealable plastic bags

measuring spoons

small plastic storage container with lid

1 Put the cucumber on the cutting board. Use the sharp knife to cut the cucumber into thin slices. On the same cutting board, use the sharp knife to cut tomatoes in half. On the cutting board, use the sharp knife to cut the turkey into ½-inch pieces.

2 Put the salad greens in the 4-cup plastic container or 1-quart resealable plastic bag. Put the lid on the container and seal or seal the bag. Put the cucumber, tomato, turkey, cheese, and, if you like, the nuts in separate small resealable plastic bags and seal. Put the salad dressing in the small plastic container. Put the lid on the container and seal. Chill all ingredients for up to 4 hours.

3 When ready to eat, uncover all ingredients. Add the cucumber, tomato, turkey, cheese, and nuts (if using) to the salad greens. Pour dressing over the salad in the container or bag. Put the lid on the container and seal or seal the bag. Shake to mix. Makes 1 serving.

Nutrition Facts per serving: 169 calories, 10 g total fat, 41 mg cholesterol, 435 mg sodium, 8 g carbohydrate, 3 g sugar, 13 g protein, 1 g fiber.

Get Moving

Jump up and down like a grasshopper 10 times.

Flick and Dot know foods from the garden make a great meal. Eat this one before these bugs start to munch on your lunch.

Fish Are Our Friends FLATBREADS

WITH THIS VITAMIN- AND VEGGIE-PACKED WRAP, YOU WON'T BE A MINDLESS EATING MACHINE EITHER, BUT YOU'RE SURE TO MAKE A SPLASH AT LUNCH!

INGREDIENTS

- ¼ cup tub-style light cream cheese
- 2 tablespoons shredded reduced-fat cheddar cheese
- 2 multigrain oval wraps or square flax roll-ups
- 2 slices cooked ham
- 1 cup mixed salad greens (romaine lettuce, iceberg lettuce, carrots, red cabbage, radishes, and snow peas)

1. Put the cream cheese and cheddar cheese in the small bowl. Stir with the wooden spoon until well mixed.

2. Use the table knife to spread the cream cheese mixture onto the wraps or roll-ups. Top each with a ham slice. Top with salad greens.

3. Roll up wraps or roll-ups. Wrap tightly in plastic wrap and chill in the refrigerator for up to 24 hours. Makes 2 servings.

Nutrition Facts per serving: 235 calories, 11 g total fat, 36 mg cholesterol, 961 mg sodium, 22 g carbohydrate, 4 g sugar, 9 g fiber, 19 g protein.

UTENSILS

- measuring cups
- measuring spoons
- small bowl
- wooden spoon
- table knife
- plastic wrap

Food Facts

Cheddar cheese can range in color from white to pumpkin orange. White is the natural color of cheddar, but it's often colored to look orange.

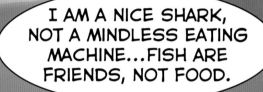

THE SKY IS FALLING APPLES! WRAPS

INGREDIENTS

- 1 small banana, peeled
- ⅓ cup crunchy peanut butter
- 4 7- to 8-inch whole wheat or white flour tortillas
- 1 cup chopped apple

1 Put the banana in the bowl. Mash with the fork. Add the peanut butter to the mashed banana. Stir with the wooden spoon to mix.

2 Use the table knife to spread peanut butter mixture over tortillas. Sprinkle with apple. Tightly roll up tortillas. Use the sharp knife to cut each roll-up in half. Wrap tightly in plastic wrap. Chill in the refrigerator for up to 24 hours. Makes 4 servings.

Nutrition Facts per serving (2 halves): 297 calories, 14 g total fat, 0 mg cholesterol, 407 mg sodium, 30 g carbohydrate, 10 g sugar, 13 g fiber, 14 g protein.

UTENSILS

- medium bowl
- fork
- measuring cups
- wooden spoon
- table knife
- sharp knife
- plastic wrap

Check This Out

Bananas are the most popular fruit in America. On average an American eats 33 pounds of bananas each year.

BODY SHOP
BLACK BEAN SALAD

INGREDIENTS

1   15-ounce can black beans

½   of a small yellow or green sweet pepper

¼   cup grape or cherry tomatoes

4   whole grain tortilla chips

1   cup packaged torn mixed salad greens

2   tablespoons shredded reduced-fat cheddar cheese

2   tablespoons purchased salsa

UTENSILS

can opener

measuring cups

colander

cutting board

sharp knife

4-cup plastic storage container with lid or 1-quart resealable plastic bag

measuring spoons

small resealable plastic bags

small plastic storage container with lid

2 small spoons

1   Use the can opener to carefully open the black beans. Measure out ¼ cup of the beans (save the rest of the beans for another use). Put the colander in the sink. Put the ¼ cup beans in the colander. Rinse beans with cold water and let the water drain into the sink. Save beans until Step 3.

2   Put the sweet pepper on the cutting board. Use the sharp knife to cut the sweet pepper into bite-size pieces. On the same cutting board, use the sharp knife to cut tomatoes into bite-size pieces. Put the pepper pieces and tomato pieces in the 4-cup plastic container or 1-quart resealable plastic bag. Put the lid on the container and seal or seal the bag. Break enough of the tortilla chips into small pieces to equal 2 tablespoons.

3   Put the drained black beans, tortilla chip pieces, salad greens, and cheese in separate small resealable bags. Seal bags. Put the salsa in the small plastic container. Put the lid on the container and seal. Chill all ingredients for up to 6 hours.

4   When ready to eat, add the black beans, tortilla pieces, salad greens, and cheese to the pepper and tomato pieces. Toss gently with the small spoons (or seal bag and shake gently to mix). Pour the salsa over the salad in the container or bag. Put the lid on the container and seal or seal the bag. Shake to mix. Makes 1 serving.

Nutrition Facts per serving: 158 calories, 3 g total fat, 10 mg cholesterol, 427 mg sodium, 22 g carbohydrate, 5 g sugar, 7 g fiber, 10 g protein.

Food Facts

Green sweet peppers have even more vitamin C than oranges and other citrus fruits.

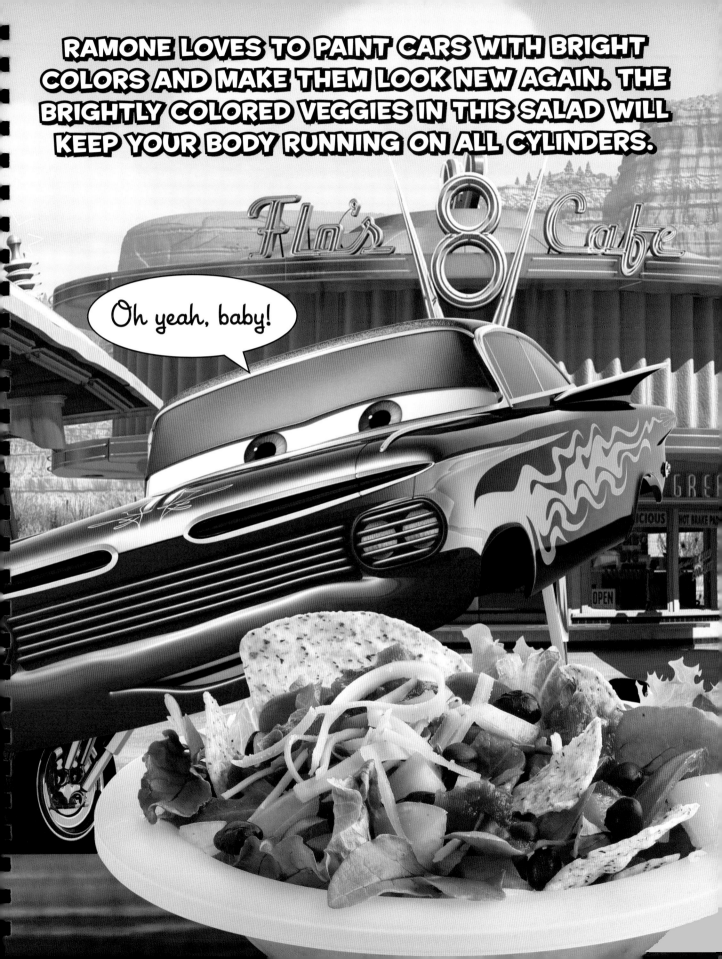

PIRATE ISLAND Tuna Boats

INGREDIENTS

1 small red or yellow sweet pepper

1 cucumber

1 3-ounce pouch tuna (water pack)

2 tablespoons light mayonnaise

1 teaspoon yellow mustard

1 recipe Baked Pita Wedges (see recipe, right)

UTENSILS

cutting board

sharp knife

plastic wrap

small spoon

small bowl

measuring cups

measuring spoons

wooden spoon

3 plastic storage containers with lids

spoon

serrated knife

pastry brush

baking sheet

hot pads

wire cooling rack

1 Put pepper on cutting board. Use the sharp knife to cut the pepper in half, cutting through the stem. Remove the stem, white membranes, and seeds from each pepper half. Save pepper until Step 4.

2 Put the cucumber on the cutting board. Use the sharp knife to cut off about one-third of the cucumber. (Wrap the remaining cucumber in plastic wrap and save it for another time.) Cut the cucumber piece in half lengthwise. Use the small spoon to scrape out the seeds from each half; throw the seeds away. Chop the cucumber (you should have about $^1/_2$ cup).

3 Open the tuna pouch. Put tuna in the bowl. Add the cucumber, mayonnaise, and mustard to the tuna. Stir with the wooden spoon until well mixed. Put the tuna mixture and pepper halves in separate storage containers. Put the lids on the storage containers and seal. Cover and chill in the refrigerator for up to 24 hours.

4 To serve, spoon half of the tuna mixture into each pepper half. Add 2 pita wedges to each pepper half for the "sail" of the boat. Serve with remaining pita wedges. Makes 2 servings.

Baked Pita Wedges: Turn on the oven to 375°F. Use the serrated knife to split 1 whole wheat pita bread round in half crosswise; split each pita half in half horizontally. Use the pastry brush to brush the cut sides of the pita pieces with 1 tablespoon olive oil. Sprinkle with $^1/_2$ teaspoon lemon-pepper seasoning. Cut each pita piece into 4 wedges. Arrange the wedges, sprinkled sides up, on the baking sheet. Put the baking sheet in the oven. Bake for 8 to 10 minutes or until wedges start to brown. Turn off oven. Use hot pads to remove the baking sheet from the oven. Put baking sheet on the wire rack. Let wedges cool. Keep the pita wedges in a covered storage container at room temperature for up to 3 days. Makes 16 wedges.

Nutrition Facts per serving: 276 calories, 13 g total fat, 25 mg cholesterol, 754 mg sodium, 28 g carbohydrate, 6 g sugar, 4 g fiber, 15 g protein.

Check This Out

Fish is good for your brain! The zinc in fish helps your thinking and memory.

Set sail on a lunchtime adventure. Pack these tuna boats and enjoy them at school, at home, or even in Neverland!

DON'T BE A CHICKEN! CUPS

IF YOUR STOMACH IS ROARING FROM HUNGER, DON'T BE AFRAID TO TRY THESE STUFFED CUPS TO FILL IT UP!

INGREDIENTS

- ½ cup light mayonnaise
- ½ teaspoon dried dillweed or lemon-pepper seasoning
- 1 9-ounce package frozen chopped cooked chicken breast, thawed
- ¾ cup chopped broccoli
- ¼ cup purchased shredded carrot
- 28 to 32 baked scoop-shape tortilla chips

UTENSILS

measuring cups
measuring spoons
small bowl
wooden spoon
medium bowl
4 plastic storage containers with lids

1 Put mayonnaise and dillweed in the small bowl. Stir with the wooden spoon to mix.

2 Put chicken, broccoli, and carrot in the medium bowl. Pour mayonnaise mixture over chicken; toss to coat. Divide chicken mixture among the 4 storage containers. Cover and chill in the refrigerator for up to 24 hours. Serve in baked tortilla chips. Makes 4 servings.

Nutrition Facts per serving: 203 calories, 11 g total fat, 44 mg cholesterol, 430 mg sodium, 10 g carbohydrate, 2 g sugar, 1 g fiber, 17 g protein.

Get Mov!ng

Sit down and stand up 10 times. Each time you stand up, do a silly dance. See how silly you can get by the tenth time!

SALAD in a POCKET

WHO SAID A SALAD HAS TO BE EATEN IN A BOWL? THIS ONE IS STUFFED INTO A PITA, SO YOU DON'T EVEN NEED A FORK!

INGREDIENTS

- **1** **large whole wheat pita bread round**
- **2** **ounces sliced cooked turkey breast**
- **½** **of a small tomato**
- **¾** **cup packaged torn iceberg lettuce mix or Caesar salad mix**
- **2** **tablespoons bottled reduced-calorie ranch salad dressing**

UTENSILS

cutting board
sharp knife
medium bowl
measuring cups
measuring spoons
wooden spoon

Nutrition Facts per serving: 167 calories, 5 g total fat, 20 mg cholesterol, 398 mg sodium, 20 g carbohydrate, 2 g sugar, 3 g fiber, 12 g protein.

1 Put the pita round on the cutting board. Use the sharp knife to cut the pita bread round in half crosswise. Using your fingers, carefully split open each half to form a pocket (be careful not to break it into 2 pieces). Save pita halves for Step 3.

2 Put the turkey on the cutting board. Use the sharp knife to cut the turkey into bite-size pieces. Put the turkey in the medium bowl. Put the tomato on the cutting board. Use the sharp knife to cut the tomato into small pieces. Add the tomato pieces to the turkey in the bowl. Add lettuce mix and salad dressing to the bowl with the turkey and the tomatoes. Stir with the wooden spoon until well mixed.

3 Spoon about half of the mixture into each pita pocket. Serve right away. Makes 2 servings.

Tip: If packing this for a take-along lunch, prepare as above through Step 2, except do not add the salad dressing to the lettuce mixture. Put the salad dressing in a small storage container with a lid. Chill salad dressing until ready to eat pita. Stir the dry lettuce mixture with the wooden spoon. Spoon half of the mixture into each pita pocket. Put the stuffed pitas in plastic containers with lids or resealable plastic bags. Chill in the refrigerator for up to 6 hours. Uncover the dressing and pour over the mixture in the pita pockets before eating.

Pop Quiz

At school you never know when the teacher will surprise you with a pop quiz. This quick quiz is all about food and activity. And it's easy if you read the first chapter of this book. Give it a try. Good luck!

1. **Which food belongs in the Grain Group?**
   A. Ice cream
   B. Cottage cheese
   C. Apple
   D. Whole wheat bread

2. **Whole grains are healthier than refined grains.**
   A. True
   B. False

3. **Which foods are good sources of calcium?**
   A. Milk
   B. Cheese
   C. Turkey
   D. Yogurt

4. **You should try to eat foods from each food group every day.**
   A. True
   B. False

5. **Which drinks should you choose?**
   A. Soda
   B. Milk
   C. Water
   D. Fruit-flavored drink

6. **Which activities count as physical activity?**
   A. Dancing
   B. Watching TV
   C. Playing video games
   D. Playing soccer

7. **How many cups of fruit should kids eat every day?**
   A. ½
   B. 1½
   C. 3
   D. 20

8. **What foods are in the produce area of the supermarket?**
   A. Canned foods
   B. Meat and fish
   C. Fresh fruit and vegetables
   D. Pasta

take a dip lunch

INGREDIENTS

- 1 **ounce smoked turkey sausage**
- 1 **ounce mozzarella or provolone cheese**
- 1 **ounce Italian bread**

  Assorted dippers such as zucchini slices, carrot sticks, small broccoli florets, sweet pepper pieces, and/or grape or cherry tomatoes

- ¼ **cup pizza sauce**

1 Put the sausage on the cutting board. Use the sharp knife to cut sausage into bite-size slices. On the same cutting board, use the sharp knife to cut the cheese into bite-size pieces. On the cutting board, use the sharp knife to cut the bread into bite-size pieces.

2 Put sausage, cheese, bread, and whatever dippers you like into the plastic container or the resealable plastic bag. Put the lid on the container and seal or seal the bag. Chill in the refrigerator for 1 to 6 hours.

3 Put the pizza sauce in the small container. Put the lid on the container and seal. Chill pizza sauce in the refrigerator for 1 to 6 hours.

4 To eat, dip the sausage, cheese, bread, and vegetable pieces into the pizza sauce. Makes 1 serving.

UTENSILS

- **cutting board**
- **sharp knife**
- **measuring cups**
- **2-cup plastic storage container with lid or 1-quart resealable plastic bag**
- **small container with lid**

Nutrition Facts per serving: 227 calories, 9 g total fat, 37 mg cholesterol, 786 mg sodium, 23 g carbohydrate, 2 g sugar, 3 g fiber, 16 g protein.

Food Facts

Italian bread and French baguettes are the same except for their shape. Italian bread is shorter and fatter than French baguettes.

BUGS LOVE A PICNIC LUNCH, ESPECIALLY WHEN THERE ARE GARDEN VEGGIES IN IT. WHETHER YOU'RE ON A PICNIC OR AT THE SCHOOL LUNCH TABLE, EAT THIS PORTABLE LUNCH BEFORE THE ANTS GET TO IT.

After School SNACKS

Yikes! Planet Earth is in big trouble, and only you and Buzz Lightyear can save the day!

But wait! How can you save the world if your stomach is rumbling? What if the alien force hears it? OR what if you become so hungry that you can't think straight, and suddenly you and Buzz are blasting off into parts unknown? Your only hope will be the cavalry—in the form of Woody and Bullseye! Luckily this doesn't have to happen if you grab a quick snack. This chapter is loaded with fun, healthy snacks that will help you operate at peak performance and save the world!

As Buzz Lightyear says, you'll be able to go "to infinity and beyond!"

I CAN'T BELIEVE I ATE THE BOWL! DIP

INGREDIENTS

1 small green or red sweet pepper

2 tablespoons fat-free refried beans

2 tablespoons purchased salsa

1 tablespoon shredded reduced-fat cheddar cheese

6 packaged peeled baby carrots or 8 baked tortilla chips

UTENSILS

cutting board
sharp knife
storage container
measuring spoons
microwave-safe custard cup
small spoon
waxed paper
hot pads

1 Put the pepper on the cutting board. Use the sharp knife to cut the pepper in half. Put one half of the pepper in the storage container and save for another use. Remove the seeds and membranes from the other pepper half. Save pepper half until Step 3.

2 Put the beans and salsa in the custard cup. Stir with the spoon to mix. Cover the custard cup with the waxed paper. Put in microwave oven and cook on 100% power (high) for 20 to 30 seconds or until heated through. Use the hot pads to remove the custard cup from the microwave oven.

3 Spoon the bean mixture into the pepper half. Sprinkle with the cheese. Dip the carrots or tortilla chips into the mixture in pepper. Makes 1 serving.

 Nutrition Facts per serving: 85 calories, 2 g total fat, 5 mg cholesterol, 349 mg sodium, 15 g carbohydrate, 7 g sugar, 4 g fiber, 4 g protein.

Food Facts

As sweet peppers mature, their color changes from green to yellow to red and finally to brown. They also become sweeter as they grow.

EYE-POPPIN' POPCORN

INGREDIENTS

1   100-calorie package microwave popcorn

2   teaspoons Cinnamon-Chocolate Seasoning, 1 tablespoon Parmesan-Ranch Seasoning, or 2 teaspoons Pizza Seasoning (see recipes, right)

UTENSILS

measuring spoons
small bowls
small spoons
measuring cups
clean small jar or container with lid

1 Pop popcorn in microwave oven following the package directions. Carefully open bag. Add the Cinnamon-Chocolate Seasoning or the Parmesan-Ranch Seasoning or the Pizza Seasoning. Close the bag and shake. Makes 1 serving (5 to 6 cups popcorn).

Cinnamon-Chocolate Seasoning: Put one 4-serving-size package sugar-free fat-free chocolate-flavored instant pudding and pie filling mix and 4 teaspoons ground cinnamon in the small bowl. Stir with the spoon to mix. Pour the mixture into the jar or container. Cover with the lid and seal tightly. Store at room temperature for up to 6 months. Makes about 6 tablespoons (enough for 9 snack servings).

Parmesan-Ranch Seasoning: Put $1/4$ cup shredded Parmesan cheese and 1 envelope ranch salad dressing mix in the small bowl. Stir with the spoon to mix. Pour the mixture into the jar or container. Cover with the lid and seal tightly. Store in the refrigerator for up to 6 months. Makes $1/2$ cup (enough for 8 snack servings).

Pizza Seasoning: Put $1/2$ cup Parmesan cheese and 2 tablespoons dried Italian seasoning, crushed, in the small bowl. Stir with the spoon to mix. Pour the mixture into the jar or container. Cover with the lid and seal tightly. Store in the refrigerator for up to 6 months. Makes 10 tablespoons (enough for 15 snack servings).

Nutrition Facts per serving with **Cinnamon-Chocolate Seasoning:** 128 calories, 2 g total fat, 0 mg cholesterol, 465 mg sodium, 28 g carbohydrate, 0 g sugar, 5 g fiber, 3 g protein.

Nutrition Facts per serving with **Parmesan-Ranch Seasoning:** 166 calories, 3 g total fat, 2 mg cholesterol, 578 mg sodium, 25 g carbohydrate, 0 g sugar, 4 g fiber, 4 g protein.

Nutrition Facts per serving with **Pizza Seasoning:** 122 calories, 3 g total fat, 2 mg cholesterol, 361 mg sodium, 24 g carbohydrate, 0 g sugar, 4 g fiber, 4 g protein.

Get Moving

Run up your stairs, do 10 jumping jacks, then go back down the stairs. Repeat.

This snack will open your eyes
to new popcorn flavors.

PIT STOP

PORTABLE PIZZA

RUNNING ON EMPTY? FILL YOUR TANK WITH THIS SPIN ON THE ULTIMATE ITALIAN FOOD!

INGREDIENTS

- **2 tablespoons purchased pizza sauce**
- **1 100-calorie package cheese-flavored crisps**
- **1 tablespoon shredded part-skim mozzarella cheese**

UTENSILS

measuring spoons
microwave-safe custard cup
waxed paper
hot pads
scissors
small spoon

1. Put pizza sauce in the custard cup. Cover with waxed paper. Put in microwave oven and cook on 100% power (high) about 20 seconds or until warm. Use hot pads to remove the custard cup from the microwave.

2. Open the package of cheese crisps. Use the scissors to cut off more of the top of the package to make it easier to eat with a spoon. Spoon pizza sauce over crackers in bag. Sprinkle with cheese. Makes 1 serving.

Nutrition Facts per serving: 133 calories, 4 g total fat, 4 mg cholesterol, 423 mg sodium, 19 g carbohydrate, 3 g sugar, 2 g fiber, 4 g protein.

Food Facts

It takes about 10 pounds of milk to make 1 pound of cheese.

Magical Fairy Wands

INGREDIENTS

Nonstick cooking spray

1 16-ounce loaf frozen whole wheat bread dough, thawed

2 egg whites

½ teaspoon water

Food coloring

Coarse salt

1 8-ounce can pizza sauce, heated,* or ⅔ cup light mayonnaise mixed with 1 tablespoon yellow mustard

UTENSILS

2 baking sheets
measuring spoons
small bowl
fork
very small bowls
spoons
clean small paintbrushes
hot pads
wire cooling rack

1 Turn on the oven to 350°F. Lightly coat the baking sheets with nonstick cooking spray. Save until Step 3.

2 Use your fingers to divide the dough into 16 pieces. Roll each dough piece into a rope that is about 10 inches long and slightly narrower at one end. If the dough springs back, let it rest for a couple of minutes and roll again.

3 Arrange the ropes about 1 inch apart on the prepared baking sheets. Put egg whites and the water in the small bowl. Stir with the fork to mix. Divide the egg white mixture among the very small bowls and tint the mixture in each bowl with food coloring to make colors you like. Use the paintbrushes to brush the egg white mixture onto the dough ropes until painted as you like. Sprinkle each dough rope lightly with coarse salt.

4 Put baking sheets in oven. Bake for 10 to 12 minutes or until dough ropes start to brown. Turn off oven. Use the hot pads to remove the baking sheets from the oven. Put on the wire rack.

5 Serve with warmed pizza sauce or with the mixture of mayonnaise and mustard. Makes 16 wands.

*Note: To heat the pizza sauce, place in a small microwave-safe bowl; cover bowl with waxed paper. Place in microwave oven and cook on 100% power (high) about 1 minute or until warm.

Nutrition Facts per wand and 2 teaspoons pizza sauce: 89 calories, 2 g total fat, 26 mg cholesterol, 339 mg sodium, 15 g carbohydrate, 1 g sugar, 1 g fiber, 4 g protein.

Get Moving

Go rollerblading with your family and friends.

Create some magic after school by making your own Fairy Wands. You even get to choose the color!

Jungle Fruit Pops

INGREDIENTS

1   cup guava nectar

1   cup unsweetened pineapple juice

1   cup fresh pineapple chunks

1   cup coarsely chopped or sliced fresh fruit such as strawberries, kiwifruit, papaya, and/or melon

UTENSILS

measuring cups

blender

12 frozen treat molds or twelve 4- to 6-ounce paper cups

foil (if using paper cups)

sharp knife (if using paper cups)

12 pop sticks (if using paper cups)

IS YOUR BRAIN DRAINED FROM A LONG DAY AT SCHOOL? USE THESE FROZEN, FRUITY POPS TO CHILL OUT!

1   Put the guava nectar, pineapple juice, and fresh pineapple chunks in the blender. Cover and blend until smooth. Divide chopped or sliced fruit among the frozen treat molds or 4- to 6-ounce paper cups. Pour the blended mixture over the fruit.

2   Add handles and cover the frozen treat molds. (Or cover each paper cup with foil. Make a small hole in the foil with the knife. Insert a pop stick into the cup through hole.) Freeze about 4 hours or until firm. Makes 12 pops.

Nutrition Facts per pop: 36 calories, 0 g total fat, 0 mg cholesterol, 1 mg sodium, 8 g carbohydrate, 7 g sugar, 0 g fiber, 0 g protein.

Boredom Busters!

"MOM, I'M BORED!" SOUND FAMILIAR? IT'S EASY TO GET BORED, ESPECIALLY WHEN THE WEATHER OUTSIDE IS LOUSY OR YOUR FRIENDS AREN'T AROUND. BUT IF YOU THINK ABOUT IT, THERE ARE TONS OF FUN THINGS YOU CAN DO. YOU CAN MAKE UP A GAME, CREATE A MAZE IN YOUR ROOM TO CLIMB AROUND, OR MAKE A FORT OUT OF OLD SHEETS. YOU'RE ONLY LIMITED BY YOUR IMAGINATION! TO BEAT BOREDOM BEFORE IT STRIKES, START BY MAKING A LIST OF THINGS YOU CAN DO. CHECK OUT THE IDEAS BELOW OR COME UP WITH NEW IDEAS OF YOUR OWN.

ACTIVITIES I CAN DO WHEN IT'S RAINING OUTSIDE:

1. _____
2. _____
3. _____
4. _____

IDEAS

- DANCE TO YOUR FAVORITE SONG
- MAKE YOUR OWN FITNESS ROUTINE TO MUSIC
- SET UP A SCAVENGER HUNT WITH FRIENDS, SIBLINGS, OR PARENTS

ACTIVITIES I CAN DO WHEN IT'S REALLY HOT OUTSIDE:

1. _____
2. _____
3. _____
4. _____

IDEAS

- RUN THROUGH A SPRINKLER
- GO SWIMMING
- GO HIKING ON A SHADY TRAIL

ACTIVITIES I CAN DO WITH MY FRIENDS:

1. _____
2. _____
3. _____
4. _____

IDEAS

- PLAY SOCCER OR KICKBALL
- PLAY A GAME OF TAG
- PLAY VOLLEYBALL

ACTIVITIES I CAN DO WHEN MY FRIENDS AREN'T AROUND:

1. _____
2. _____
3. _____
4. _____

IDEAS

- JUMP ROPE OR SWING
- HULA HOOP AND TIME YOURSELF TO SEE HOW LONG YOU CAN GO
- SHOOT SOME HOOPS

Buenos Apple Nachos

INGREDIENTS

1   small apple

2   or 3 strawberries

1   tablespoon peanut butter

1   tablespoon shredded or flaked coconut (if you like)

1   tablespoon vanilla low-fat yogurt

UTENSILS

cutting board

sharp knife

serving plate

measuring spoons

microwave-safe custard cup or small bowl

hot pads

small spoon

1 Put apple on the cutting board with the stem side up. Use the sharp knife to cut the apple into slices, starting from a rounded side and cutting toward the core. Repeat from other side. Throw away the core. Arrange apple slices on the serving plate. Save until Step 3. Put the strawberries on the cutting board and use the sharp knife to cut off their green tops. Chop the strawberries. Save until Step 3.

2 Put peanut butter in the custard cup. Put in microwave oven and cook on 100% power (high) about 20 seconds or until peanut butter is thin, but not bubbly. Remove using the hot pads.

3 Spoon the peanut butter over apples on plate. Sprinkle with strawberries. If you like, sprinkle with the coconut. Top with yogurt. Makes 1 or 2 servings.

Nutrition Facts per serving: 186 calories, 9 g total fat, 1 mg cholesterol, 85 mg sodium, 26 g carbohydrate, 19 g sugar, 5 g fiber, 5 g protein.

Check This Out

There are more than 7,000 varieties of apples!

Ron never seems to get enough nachos. They don't serve these at Bueno Nacho, but Ron still thinks they are totally badical.

Hiking Trail GRANOLA BARS

INGREDIENTS

Nonstick cooking spray

1   cup low-fat granola
1   cup rolled oats
1/2   cup whole wheat flour
1   egg
1/3   cup canola oil
1/3   cup honey
1/2   teaspoon ground cinnamon

UTENSILS

8×8-inch baking pan
foil
measuring cups
large bowl
wooden spoon
measuring spoons
hot pads
wire cooling rack
cutting board
sharp knife

1 Turn on the oven to 325°F. Line the baking pan with foil, letting foil go up a little bit over the edges of the pan. Lightly coat the foil with nonstick cooking spray. Save until Step 2.

2 Put the granola, oats, and flour in the large bowl. Stir with the wooden spoon to mix. Add the egg, oil, honey, and cinnamon. Stir with the wooden spoon until all of the ingredients are coated. Press evenly into the prepared baking pan.

3 Put the baking pan in the oven. Bake for 30 to 35 minutes or until lightly browned around the edges. Turn off oven. Use the hot pads to remove the pan from the oven. Put the pan on the wire rack. Cool baked mixture in the pan for 2 hours. Grasp ends of foil and carefully remove from the pan. Put on the cutting board. Remove the foil and throw it away. Use the sharp knife to cut the baked mixture into bars. Makes 12 bars.

Nutrition Facts per bar: 190 calories, 8 g total fat, 18 mg cholesterol, 29 mg sodium, 27 g carbohydrate, 11 g sugar, 3 g fiber, 4 g protein.

Get Moving Get funky! Find some fast songs on the radio and start dancing.

Whether you've been hiking a trail or just the hallways at school, these bars will fill you up with energy!

Ride the Tide Dip

INGREDIENTS

1   6- to 8-ounce container lemon low-fat yogurt

Dash ground ginger

¹/₂   cup fresh strawberries

2   cups assorted fresh fruit such as apple and/or pear wedges, plum slices, and/or seedless grapes

UTENSILS

small bowl
large spoon
measuring cups
cutting board
sharp knife
medium bowl
potato masher
serving bowl
small spoon
thin table knife or thin metal spatula
serving plate

1 Put the yogurt and ginger in the small bowl. Stir with the large spoon to mix. Save until Step 3.

2 Put the strawberries on the cutting board. Use the sharp knife to cut the green tops off of the strawberries. Put the strawberries in the medium bowl. Use the potato masher to mash the berries well.

3 Spoon the yogurt mixture into the serving bowl. Use the small spoon to drop small spoonfuls of mashed strawberries over the yogurt mixture. Using the thin knife or spatula, gently swirl the mashed berries into the yogurt mixture. Arrange the fresh fruit on the serving plate. Serve fruit with swirled yogurt mixture. (Cover and chill any remaining yogurt mixture for up to 24 hours.) Makes 4 servings.

 Nutrition Facts per serving: 87 calories, 1 g total fat, 2 mg cholesterol, 26 mg sodium, 20 g carbohydrate, 16 g sugar, 2 g fiber, 2 g protein.

Food Facts

Pears are different than most other fruits because they ripen better once they're off the tree.

Dip your favorite fruit dunkers into this righteous recipe for a snack that's totally sweet!
You so totally rock, Squirt! So gimme some fin!
Whoa! That was so cool! Hey, Dad! Did you see that? Did you see me? Did you see what I did?

(((MISSION: DINNER)))

Yay! School's out for the day! Time to rest and relax. What? No time to rest and relax? What's the sitch?

The sitch is that you're probably still on the go. You might not have villains to fight, like Kim Possible and her goofball boyfriend, Ron. But your stuff is just as important, like after-school clubs, sports practice, music lessons, and homework.

Don't worry. We have the perfect solution to make your evening so not the drama. And that's the perfect dinner! Share these recipes with your folks and have fun making the recipes together. You'll quickly discover that dinner doesn't have to be a mission impossible.

Be Our Guest Berry Salad

INGREDIENTS

¹/₄	cup orange juice
1	tablespoon salad oil
2	teaspoons honey mustard or Dijon-style mustard
1	teaspoon sugar
¹/₄	teaspoon salt
4	cups torn lettuce
1¹/₂	cups fresh blueberries, raspberries, quartered strawberries, and/or canned mandarin orange sections, drained
2	tablespoons bite-size cheddar fish-shape or pretzel crackers

UTENSILS

measuring cups
measuring spoons
screw-top jar with lid
medium bowl
tongs for tossing
4 salad plates

1 To make the dressing, put the orange juice, oil, mustard, sugar, and salt in the screw-top jar. Tightly cover with the lid. Shake until combined. Put the lettuce in the medium bowl. Drizzle the dressing over the lettuce. Using the tongs, gently toss the lettuce to coat with the dressing. Divide the lettuce among the salad plates.

2 Put the fruit on the lettuce. Sprinkle with the crackers. Serve immediately. Makes 4 side-dish servings.

 Nutrition Facts per serving: 86 calories, 4 g total fat, 0 mg cholesterol, 208 mg sodium, 13 g carbohydrate, 8 g sugar, 3 g fiber, 1 g protein.

Food Facts

Raspberries can be red, black, or gold. Each berry is actually hundreds of individual fruits, each one with a seed.

THIS SALAD MAKES A FUN SIDE DISH, BUT IF YOU HAVE A BEAST-SIZE HUNGER, TRY ADDING SOME CHICKEN TO THIS BERRY DELICIOUS SALAD FOR AN ENCHANTED MEAL.

CHILI-TOPPED Potato Wedges

INGREDIENTS

2 russet potatoes

1/4 teaspoon salt

1 tablespoon water

1 medium tomato

1 15- to 16-ounce can vegetarian chili

1/2 cup shredded reduced-fat cheddar cheese (2 ounces)

UTENSILS

vegetable brush
cutting board
sharp knife
microwave-safe 2-quart square baking dish
measuring spoons
waxed paper
hot pads
tongs
fork
can opener
small saucepan
rubber scraper
wooden spoon
wire cooling rack
4 serving plates
measuring cups

1 Scrub the potatoes with the vegetable brush. Put potatoes on the cutting board. Use the knife to cut potatoes in half lengthwise. Cut each potato half into 4 pieces lengthwise (you should have 16 potato wedges). Arrange the potato wedges in the baking dish. Sprinkle the potatoes with the salt. Add the water to the bottom of the baking dish. Cover baking dish with waxed paper. Put the dish in the microwave and cook on 100% power (high) for 9 to 10 minutes or until potatoes are done. Stop the microwave 3 times during cooking and use the hot pads to remove the dish from the microwave and the tongs to rearrange the potato wedges in the dish. The potatoes are done when they are tender when you pierce them with the fork.

2 Meanwhile, put the tomato on the cutting board and chop the tomato with the sharp knife. Save until Step 3. Use the can opener to open the chili. Put the chili in the saucepan, scraping sides of can with the rubber scraper. Put the saucepan on the burner. Turn the burner to medium heat. Cook until mixture is heated through, stirring now and then with the wooden spoon. Turn off burner.

3 Use the hot pads to remove the potatoes from the microwave. Put the baking dish on the wire rack. Use the tongs to remove the potatoes from the baking dish and put them on the serving plates. Top each with chili and sprinkle with cheese and tomato. Makes 4 servings.

Nutrition Facts per serving: 195 calories, 4 g total fat, 10 mg cholesterol, 609 mg sodium, 30 g carbohydrate, 5 g sugar, 6 g fiber, 11 g protein.

THE GARDEN GAME

The produce section of the supermarket is loaded with tons of fresh fruits and veggies. All that food had to get there somehow! Read the clues below and see if you can match the food to how it was grown before it got to the supermarket. (Hint: There is a picture of each answer.)

1. I grow best on bushes in tropical climates, and I have an outer peel that's usually yellow:

_____

2. I grow on trees and taste best in the fall, shortly after harvest from the orchard:

_____

3. I grow in the dirt, and you have to dig to find me:

_____

4. I grow on vines in the hot days of summer when I get plenty of sunshine:

_____

5. I grow best in the ground when the weather is cool; some say I look like little trees:

_____

6. I grow on small plants that are close to the ground. Even though I have a lot of seeds, I am very delicate and must be picked by hand when I'm ripe:

_____

7. I grow best in tropical weather with lots of sun. If you plant my crown, a new fruit will grow in about 18 months:

_____

8. I grow on vines in almost any climate, but temperate regions are my favorite. You'll most often find me in red and green colors:

_____

9. I grow in the ground; I'm actually a root. You'll most often find me colored orange:

_____

Pizza Planet
Cheesy Calzones

INGREDIENTS

Nonstick cooking spray

3 ounces Canadian-style bacon or cooked ham

1 13.8-ounce package refrigerated pizza dough

$1/3$ cup pizza sauce

1 cup shredded part-skim mozzarella cheese (4 ounces)

1 tablespoon fat-free milk

1 tablespoon finely shredded Parmesan cheese

Pizza sauce

UTENSILS

baking sheet
foil
cutting board
sharp knife
measuring cups
pizza cutter or sharp knife
small spoon
fork
measuring spoons
pastry brush
hot pads
wire cooling rack
wide metal spatula

1 Turn on the oven to 400°F. Line the baking sheet with foil. Lightly coat the foil with nonstick cooking spray. Save until Step 4. Put the Canadian bacon or ham on the cutting board. Use the sharp knife to chop the meat (you should have $3/4$ cup). Save until Step 3.

2 Unroll the pizza dough into a rectangle on a lightly floured surface. Using the pizza cutter or sharp knife, cut the dough rectangle in half lengthwise, then cut each half into thirds crosswise. You should have 6 rectangles.

3 Use the small spoon to spread some of the $1/3$ cup pizza sauce onto each dough rectangle. Sprinkle 1 side of each dough rectangle with some of the mozzarella cheese and some of the Canadian bacon or ham. Fold the other side of each dough rectangle over the cheese and Canadian bacon or ham. Use the fork to seal the edges. Prick the top of each calzone with the fork several times. Use the pastry brush to brush the top of each with milk and sprinkle with Parmesan cheese.

4 Arrange the calzones on the prepared baking sheet. Put the baking sheet in the oven. Bake for 12 to 14 minutes or until golden brown. Turn off oven. Use the hot pads to remove the baking sheet from the oven. Put baking sheet on the wire rack. Cool calzones on baking sheet for 10 minutes. Use the wide metal spatula to remove the calzones from the baking sheet. Serve warm with additional pizza sauce. Makes 6 calzones.

Nutrition Facts per calzone: 230 calories, 7 g total fat, 20 mg cholesterol, 711 mg sodium, 30 g carbohydrate, 4 g sugar, 2 g fiber, 12 g protein.

Pretend you're a superhero fighting evil villains and do 10 karate kicks with each leg—hiyah!

PACKED WITH MEAT, CHEESE, AND PIZZA SAUCE FOR DUNKING, THESE CALZONES ARE OUT OF THIS WORLD!

Snow Day Soup

INGREDIENTS

- **3** 14-ounce cans reduced-sodium chicken broth
- **3** cups favorite loose-pack frozen mixed vegetable blend
- **1/8** teaspoon black pepper
- **2** 6-ounce packages refrigerated cooked chicken breast strips, torn into bite-size pieces
- **1 1/2** cups packaged low-fat biscuit mix
- **1/2** cup fat-free milk

1 Use the can opener to open the chicken broth. Put broth, vegetables, and pepper in the large saucepan. Put pan on a burner. Turn the burner to medium-high heat. Cook until boiling. Turn burner to low heat. Cover and cook for 5 minutes. Stir in chicken with the wooden spoon.

2 While the broth mixture is cooking, put the biscuit mix and milk in the medium bowl. Stir with the large spoon until combined.

3 For dumplings, spoon the dough in 12 mounds on top of the hot broth mixture. Cover and cook about 10 minutes more or until a toothpick inserted into dumplings comes out clean. Turn off burner. Remove pan from burner. Makes 6 servings.

Nutrition Facts per serving: 259 calories, 5 g total fat, 40 mg cholesterol, 1,226 mg sodium, 33 g carbohydrate, 4 g sugar, 3 g fiber, 22 g protein.

UTENSILS

- can opener
- measuring cups
- measuring spoons
- large saucepan with lid
- wooden spoon
- medium bowl
- large spoon
- wooden toothpick

Check This Out

Soup is usually served hot, but some soups, such as fruit soups, taste best when served cold.

Dogs love to play, especially in the snow. This soup is topped with biscuit snowballs that will warm you up on chilly days.

Rootin' Tootin' HAM SANDWICHES

INGREDIENTS

- **2** to **3 teaspoons Dijon-style mustard**
- **4 slices firm wheat bread, white bread, or sourdough bread**
- **2 ounces thinly sliced cooked ham**
- **2 slices Swiss cheese (2 ounces total)**
- **¹⁄₄ cup fat-free milk**
- **1 egg white**
- **Nonstick cooking spray**

UTENSILS

- table knife
- measuring spoons
- measuring cups
- shallow bowl or pie plate
- whisk
- nonstick griddle or large skillet
- pancake turner

1 Use the knife to spread the mustard on 2 of the bread slices. Top mustard with ham and cheese. Place remaining bread slices on top of the ham and cheese. Put the milk and egg white in the shallow bowl or pie plate. Whisk until well mixed.

2 Coat an unheated nonstick griddle or large skillet with nonstick cooking spray. Put griddle or skillet on burner. Turn burner to medium heat. Dip each sandwich in milk mixture and turn to coat both sides. Put sandwiches on the hot griddle or in skillet. Cook for 1 to 2 minutes or until bottoms are golden brown. Use the pancake turner to turn sandwiches over. Cook for 1 to 2 minutes more or until golden brown and cheese is melted. Turn off burner. Remove griddle or skillet from burner. Use the pancake turner to remove the sandwiches from the griddle or skillet. Makes 2 servings.

 Nutrition Facts per serving: 317 calories, 13 g total fat, 43 mg cholesterol, 855 mg sodium, 31 g carbohydrate, 6 g sugar, 0 g fiber, 20 g protein.

Food Facts

Why are there holes in Swiss cheese?
When Swiss cheese is made, the bacteria that give the cheese its flavor and texture also make carbon dioxide gas, and these gas bubbles make holes in the cheese.

THESE CHEESY SANDWICHES WILL ROUND UP EVERYONE TO THE TABLE. HOT OFF THE GRIDDLE, THEY'LL KEEP YOU RUNNING 'TIL THE COWS COME HOME.

POWER UP
PASTA AND MEATBALLS

INGREDIENTS

Nonstick cooking spray

12 ounces lean ground beef

1 teaspoon dried Italian seasoning

$1/2$ teaspoon bottled minced garlic (if you like)

$1/2$ teaspoon salt

4 ounces dried multigrain rotini or penne pasta ($1^1/_2$ cups)

2 cups purchased pasta sauce

Shredded Parmesan cheese (if you like)

UTENSILS

15×10×1-inch baking pan
measuring spoons
large bowl
wooden spoon
large saucepan
colander
measuring cups
small saucepan with lid
hot pads
wire cooling rack
serving spoon
4 serving plates
tongs
large spoon

1 Turn on the oven to 375°F. Lightly coat the baking pan with nonstick cooking spray. Save until Step 2. Put the beef, Italian seasoning, garlic (if you like), and salt in the large bowl. Mix with the wooden spoon until combined. Use your hands to shape the mixture into 24 meatballs (they will each be about 1 inch in size).

2 Put the meatballs in the prepared baking pan, spacing them evenly. Wash your hands well with soap and warm water. Put the baking pan in the oven. Bake for 10 to 12 minutes or until meatballs are no longer pink inside.

3 Meanwhile, fill the large saucepan half full with water. Put saucepan on the burner. Turn the burner to high heat. When water boils, slowly add the pasta to the water. Turn the burner to medium heat. Cook the pasta for 12 minutes. Set the colander in a sink. Carefully pour pasta into the colander. Save until Step 6.

4 Put the pasta sauce in the small saucepan. Cover with the lid. Put the pan on the burner. Turn the burner to medium heat. Cook until the sauce is heated through and bubbly. Turn off burner. Remove pan from burner.

5 Turn off oven. Use hot pads to remove the pan with the meatballs from the oven. Put the pan on the wire rack.

6 Use the serving spoon to divide the pasta among the serving plates. Use the tongs to put 6 meatballs on each plate. Spoon the pasta sauce over pasta and meatballs. If you like, sprinkle with Parmesan cheese. Makes 4 servings.

Nutrition Facts per serving: 288 calories, 10 g tot[...], 54 mg cholesterol, 724 mg sodium, 28 g carbohy[...], 6 g sugar, 4 g fiber, 22 g protein.

Get Moving

Pretend you're Mr. Incredible breaking through walls. Punch the air 10 times with each arm!

BLAST OFF BURRITOS

INGREDIENTS

6   8-inch multigrain
    flour tortillas

1   6-ounce package refrigerated
    cooked chicken breast strips

1   medium tomato

1   cup loose-pack frozen
    whole kernel corn

$^2/_3$ cup purchased salsa

$1^1/_2$ cups torn mixed salad greens

$^1/_2$ cup shredded reduced-fat
    Monterey Jack cheese
    (2 ounces)

    Purchased salsa (if you like)

1 Turn on the oven to 350°F. Wrap tortillas in the foil. Put the foil-wrapped tortillas in the oven. Bake for 10 minutes. Turn off oven. Use hot pads to remove tortillas from oven. Put tortillas on the wire rack.

2 While the tortillas are baking, put the chicken on the cutting board. Use the sharp knife to cut chicken into small pieces. Save until Step 3. Chop the tomato (you should have $^3/_4$ cup). Save until Step 4.

3 Put the chicken, corn, and the $^2/_3$ cup salsa in the large skillet. Put the skillet on the burner. Turn the burner to medium heat. Cook until mixture is bubbly, stirring often with the wooden spoon. Turn off burner. Remove skillet from burner.

4 Put tortillas on work surface. Top each tortilla with some of the chicken mixture and some of the greens and tomato. Sprinkle with some of the cheese. Fold in sides of tortillas. Roll up tortillas. Cut each tortilla in half to serve. If you like, serve with additional salsa. Makes 6 servings.

Nutrition Facts per serving: 234 calories, 7 g total fat, 27 mg cholesterol, 980 mg sodium, 33 g carbohydrate, 5 g sugar, 7 g fiber, 15 g protein.

UTENSILS
foil
hot pads
wire cooling rack
cutting board
sharp knife
measuring cups
large skillet
wooden spoon

Food Facts

Corn is actually part of the grass family, so it isn't really a vegetable at all; it's a grain!

TO INFINITY AND BEYOND!

Kids and space rangers alike need to fuel up in the evening. Whether you're heading to Star Command or sports practice—or hitting the books—these burritos will help you blast off!

Secret Lair BURGERS

INGREDIENTS

- 1 pound lean ground beef
- 1/2 teaspoon salt
- 1/4 teaspoon black pepper
- 4 dill pickle slices (if you like)
- 1/2 cup shredded reduced-fat cheddar cheese (2 ounces)
- 4 whole wheat or whole grain hamburger buns
- Lettuce leaves
- Tomato slices
- Ketchup (if you like)
- Yellow mustard (if you like)

UTENSILS

- closed indoor electric grill
- measuring spoons
- large bowl
- measuring cups
- 2 wide metal spatulas
- instant-read thermometer

1 Preheat the closed indoor electric grill following the manufacturer's directions. Put the beef, salt, and pepper in the large bowl. Mix gently with your hands until combined. With your hands, divide beef mixture into 8 pieces. Flatten each piece into a patty about 3 inches in diameter. Top 4 of the patties with pickles, if you like, and then top with cheese. Put the plain patties on top of the cheese-topped patties. Use your fingers to press the edges together until sealed. Wash your hands well with soap and warm water.

2 Use a wide metal spatula to put one or two patties at a time on the indoor electric grill. Close the lid of the grill. Cook for 5 to 6 minutes or until the thermometer inserted into the centers of the burgers reads 160°F. Use a clean wide metal spatula to take the burgers off of the grill. When all the burgers are cooked, turn off the grill.

3 Serve the burgers, lettuce, and tomato in the buns. If you like, serve with ketchup and mustard. Makes 4 servings.

Nutrition Facts per serving: 345 calories, 15 g total fat, 82 mg cholesterol, 666 mg sodium, 23 g carbohydrate, 5 g sugar, 2 g fiber, 28 g protein.

In 1982, residents of Rutland, North Dakota made the world's largest hamburger. It weighed 3,591 pounds and was eaten by about 8,000 people.

Mad scientists aren't the only ones with secret lairs. You'll surprise everyone with the pickles and cheese hiding inside these burgers.

Fiesta Taco Pizza

INGREDIENTS

1	medium tomato
1	medium onion
12	ounces lean ground beef
$2/3$	cup purchased salsa
6	tostada shells
1	cup shredded reduced-fat cheddar cheese (4 ounces)
$1/2$	to 1 cup purchased shredded lettuce
	Light dairy sour cream (if you like)
	Purchased salsa (if you like)

UTENSILS

cutting board
sharp knife
measuring cups
large skillet
wooden spoon
colander
medium bowl
disposable container
baking sheet
hot pads
wire cooling rack

1 Turn on oven to 375°F. Put the tomato and onion on the cutting board. Use the sharp knife to chop the onion and tomato into small pieces (you should have $1/2$ cup onion and $3/4$ cup tomato). Save the tomato until Step 5.

2 Put the ground beef and onion in the large skillet. Break up meat with the wooden spoon. Put the skillet on a burner. Turn the burner to medium-high heat. Cook until meat is brown and the onion is tender, stirring now and then with the wooden spoon. This will take 8 to 10 minutes. Turn off burner. Remove skillet from burner.

3 Place the colander over the bowl. Spoon meat mixture into the colander and let fat drain into the bowl. Spoon meat back into skillet. Put fat into the disposable container and throw away. Stir the $2/3$ cup salsa into meat in skillet.

4 Arrange the tostada shells on the baking sheet. Spoon the meat mixture onto the shells. Sprinkle with the cheese. Put the baking sheet in the oven. Bake about 10 minutes or until the cheese is melted. Turn off oven.

5 Use the hot pads to take the baking sheet out of the oven. Set baking sheet on the wire rack. Sprinkle the pizzas with the lettuce and tomato. If you like, top each pizza with sour cream and additional salsa. Makes 6 servings.

Nutrition Facts per serving: 220 calories, 12 g total fat, 49 mg cholesterol, 401 mg sodium, 11 g carbohydrate, 2 g sugar, 1 g fiber, 16 g protein.

Check This Out

In the U.S., there are more than 60,000 pizza restaurants. Together they serve about 2.5 billion pizzas every year!

TURN DINNERTIME INTO A FIESTA! THIS PIZZA MIGHT GET MESSY, BUT IT'S SURE TO BE A FAMILY FAVORITE.

SLOPPY DOGS

INGREDIENTS

- 12 ounces lean ground beef
- 1 8-ounce can tomato sauce
- 1 tablespoon dried minced onion
- 1/4 teaspoon dried oregano, crushed
- 1/4 teaspoon dried basil, crushed
- 8 whole grain hamburger or hot dog buns
- 1 cup shredded part-skim mozzarella cheese (4 ounces)
- 1/4 cup grated Parmesan cheese
- Carrot sticks (if you like)

UTENSILS

- large skillet with a lid
- wooden spoon
- colander
- medium bowl
- disposable container
- can opener
- measuring spoons
- measuring cups

1 Put the ground beef in the skillet. Break up meat with the wooden spoon. Put the skillet on a burner. Turn the burner to medium-high heat. Cook until meat is completely browned, stirring now and then with the wooden spoon. This will take 8 to 10 minutes. Turn off burner. Remove skillet from burner.

2 Place the colander over the bowl. Spoon meat into the colander and let fat drain into the bowl. Spoon meat back into skillet. Put fat in the disposable container and throw away.

3 Use the can opener to open the tomato sauce. Add the tomato sauce, onion, oregano, and basil to meat mixture in the skillet. Put the skillet on a burner. Turn the burner to medium-high heat. Cook until the mixture comes to boiling, stirring now and then with the wooden spoon. Turn the burner to low heat. Cover with the lid and cook for 15 minutes. Turn off burner.

4 Spoon the meat mixture onto bun bottoms. Top with mozzarella cheese and Parmesan cheese. Cover with the bun tops. If you like, serve with carrot sticks. Makes 8 servings.

Nutrition Facts per serving: 291 calories, 9 g total fat, 38 mg cholesterol, 580 mg sodium, 32 g carbohydrate, 2 g sugar, 2 g fiber, 18 g protein.

Get Moving Time yourself to see how many jumping jacks you can do in one minute!

IF NEAT AND TIDY ISN'T YOUR STYLE, GET YOUR PAWS ON THESE SAUCY SLOPPY DOGS.

TO-SCREAM-FOR DESSERTS

What stands 8 feet tall, has blue fur, and tries his hardest to scare the stuffing out of you? Why, that would be Sulley, of course! And don't forget his one-eyed best friend, Mike!

But wait! Stop! Don't go running from the room screaming your head off. These guys might look scary, but really, they're just a couple of cream puffs. And to show you how sweet they really are, they've decided to share their recipes in this collection of the coolest, most stupendous desserts ever!

After all, don't forget the Monsters, Inc. motto: "We Scare Because We Care!" Or in this case—"We Share Because We Dare!"

Monstropolis Community Cookbook

Celia's Slithering Snake Birthday Cake

Monstrous Sundae

Waternoose's Chunky Chocolate Moose

So Not the Drama
Apple Pie Cups

0101001010000001010101011010
0101001010000000 01010

INGREDIENTS

1   **14-ounce snack-size container unsweetened applesauce**

$^1/_8$ **teaspoon apple pie spice or ground cinnamon**

2   **tablespoons round toasted multigrain cereal or oat square cereal**

1   **tablespoon sliced almonds, pecan pieces, or walnut pieces (if you like)**

UTENSILS

small spoons

microwave-safe 6-ounce custard cup or small bowl

measuring spoons

hot pads

small resealable plastic bag (if you like)

1 Uncover the applesauce container. Spoon applesauce into the custard cup or small bowl. Add apple pie spice. Stir with a small spoon to mix.

2 Put custard cup with applesauce in the microwave. Cook, uncovered, on 100% power (high) for 15 to 30 seconds or until warm. Use hot pads to carefully remove custard cup from microwave. Stir the applesauce.

3 If you like, put the cereal in a resealable plastic bag and use your hands to coarsely crush the cereal. Sprinkle cereal over warm applesauce. If you like, sprinkle with nuts. Eat while warm. Makes 1 serving.

Strawberry-Apple Crisp: Make as directed above, except do not add the apple pie spice to the applesauce. Instead stir 1 teaspoon low-sugar strawberry preserves into the cold applesauce. Heat and serve as directed above in steps 2 and 3.

Nutrition Facts per serving: 65 calories, 0 g total fat, 0 mg cholesterol, 25 mg sodium, 17 g carbohydrate, 13 g sugar, 2 g fiber, 0 g protein.

 Check This Out

Astronaut John Glenn, the first American to orbit Earth, carried applesauce in squeezable tubes on his first space flight.

When time is short, try this shortcut apple pie. It has unbeatable apple flavor and is ready in no time flat!
MAKE DESSERT AND FIGHT VILLAINS? NO BIG.

Play-Time Peanut Butter Treat

Chocolate and peanut butter make the perfect team for a lip-smackin' sweet treat.

INGREDIENTS

- 1 cup graham cracker crumbs
- 1/2 cup finely chopped peanuts
- 3 tablespoons butter, melted
- 1/4 cup tub-style light cream cheese
- 2 tablespoons creamy peanut butter
- 2 tablespoons fat-free milk
- 2 cups fat-free milk
- 1 4-serving-size package sugar-free chocolate-flavored instant pudding mix

UTENSILS

- measuring cups
- medium bowl
- wooden spoons
- measuring spoons
- 2 small bowls
- 2-quart square baking dish
- plastic wrap
- large bowl
- whisk
- rubber scraper
- small spoon
- thin metal spatula or table knife
- 12 dessert dishes

1 Put graham cracker crumbs and chopped peanuts in the medium bowl. Stir with a wooden spoon to mix. Stir in the melted butter until combined. Measure out 3 tablespoons of the crumb mixture and put it in a small bowl. Save until Step 3. Press the remaining crumb mixture into the bottom of the baking dish. Cover with plastic wrap and chill in the refrigerator while making the filling.

2 To make the filling, put the cream cheese and peanut butter in a small bowl. Stir with a wooden spoon until smooth. Gradually stir in the 2 tablespoons milk, stirring until smooth. Save until Step 3.

3 Put the 2 cups milk and the pudding mix in the large bowl. Whisk until combined. Continue whisking for 2 minutes. Use the rubber scraper to spread the pudding mixture over graham cracker crust in pan. Use the small spoon to drop the peanut butter mixture in small mounds onto the pudding mixture. Using a thin metal spatula or table knife, gently swirl the peanut butter mixture into the pudding mixture. Sprinkle with the reserved 3 tablespoons crumb mixture.

4 Cover with plastic wrap. Chill in the refrigerator about 2 hours or until set. To serve, spoon into the dessert dishes. Makes 12 servings.

Nutrition Facts per serving: 147 calories, 9 g total fat, 11 mg cholesterol, 247 mg sodium, 12 g carbohydrate, 3 g sugar, 1 g fiber, 5 g protein.

MONSTER SUNDAE RECIPE

SULLEY AND MIKE HAVE A MONSTER CRAVING FOR SOMETHING SWEET. INSTEAD OF CANDY AND JUNK FOOD, THEY PREFER NATURE'S DESSERT —FRESH FRUIT! FILL IN THE BLANKS BELOW TO CREATE A MONSTER-SIZE FRUIT SUNDAE FOR SULLEY AND MIKE TO EAT. REMEMBER TO INCLUDE AS MANY DIFFERENT COLORS OF FRUITS AS YOU CAN (RED, GREEN, YELLOW, BLUE, ORANGE, PURPLE) SO THEY GET EVEN MORE HEALTHY NUTRIENTS.

FIRST FIND A _____ TO MAKE THE SUNDAE IN.
(KITCHEN TOOL)

START BY PUTTING IN SOME _____ _____ TO HELP
(COLOR)   (FRUIT)

KEEP SULLEY AND MIKE HEALTHY. NEXT ADD _____ _____
(NUMBER)   (COLOR)

_____ FOR MORE VITAMINS AND MINERALS.
(FRUIT)

ADD A _____ _____ _____ FOR
(ADJECTIVE)   (COLOR)   (FRUIT)

SULLEY. IT'S ONE OF HIS FAVORITES! NOW USE A _____ TO
(KITCHEN TOOL)

CUT A _____ _____ TO ADD TO THE SUNDAE.
(COLOR)   (FRUIT)

NEXT ADD _____ CUP(S) OF _____ _____
(CUP MEASUREMENT)   (ADJECTIVE)   (FLAVOR)

LOW-FAT YOGURT TO GIVE SULLEY AND MIKE MORE CALCIUM FOR

STRONG BONES AND TEETH. FINALLY TOP THE SUNDAE WITH A

_____ _____, AND THIS SUNDAE IS SURE TO
(COLOR)   (FRUIT)

SATISFY EVEN SULLEY'S SWEET TOOTH!

DISAPPEARING Chocolate Chip Cookies

INGREDIENTS

- 1 cup rolled oats
- 1/2 cup butter, softened
- 1 cup packed brown sugar
- 1 teaspoon baking soda
- 1/4 teaspoon salt
- 1 cup plain low-fat yogurt
- 2 eggs
- 1 teaspoon vanilla
- 2 1/2 cups all-purpose flour
- 1 cup miniature semisweet chocolate pieces (6 ounces)

UTENSILS

- measuring cups
- shallow baking pan
- wooden spoon
- hot pads
- food processor or blender
- large mixing bowl
- electric mixer
- measuring spoons
- rubber scraper
- cookie sheet
- wide metal spatula
- wire cooling racks

1 Turn on the oven to 375°F. Put oats in the shallow baking pan. Put the baking pan in the oven. Bake about 10 minutes or until toasted, stirring once with the wooden spoon. Use hot pads to remove baking pan from oven. Put oats in the food processor or blender. Cover and process or blend until oats are ground. Save until Step 2.

2 Put butter in the large mixing bowl. Beat butter with the electric mixer on medium to high speed for 30 seconds. Add brown sugar, baking soda, and salt. Beat until combined, stopping the mixer occasionally and scraping the sides with the rubber scraper. Add the yogurt, eggs, and vanilla and beat until combined. Beat in as much of the flour as you can with the mixer. Stop the mixer. Stir in the oats and any remaining flour with the wooden spoon. Stir in chocolate pieces.

3 Drop dough by rounded teaspoons onto the ungreased cookie sheet. Fill the cookie sheet with mounds of dough, leaving about 2 inches between cookies. Put the cookie sheet in the oven. Bake for 9 to 11 minutes or until cookie bottoms are browned. Use the hot pads to remove cookie sheet from oven. Use the wide spatula to transfer cookies to the wire rack; let cookies cool. Repeat with remaining dough, letting cookie sheet cool between batches or using a second cookie sheet. Turn off oven. Makes about 60 cookies.

Nutrition Facts per cookie: 71 calories, 3 g total fat, 12 mg cholesterol, 49 mg sodium, 11 g carbohydrate, 6 g sugar, 0 g fiber, 1 g protein.

Food Facts

Rolled oats are oat groats that have been steamed and flattened with giant rollers.

Unless you can put a force field around them, these cookies are sure to disappear.

Princess Pretzel Parfaits

INGREDIENTS

- 1   18-ounce tub light cream cheese, softened
- 1   tablespoon fat-free milk
- 1   teaspoon vanilla
- 1   cup coarsely crushed pretzels (about 2¼ ounces)
- 1½   cups sliced fresh strawberries
- 4   whole pretzels (if you like)

UTENSILS

measuring spoons
small bowl
wooden spoon
measuring cups
four 8-ounce parfait or drinking glasses
small spoon
plastic wrap (if chilling)

1 Put cream cheese, milk, and vanilla in the small bowl. Stir with the wooden spoon until smooth. Divide half of the crushed pretzels among the parfait glasses or drinking glasses. Spoon half of the cream cheese mixture over pretzels. Layer half of the strawberries over cream cheese mixture. Repeat layers. Serve immediately or cover with plastic wrap and chill in the refrigerator for up to 4 hours before serving. If you like, top each serving with a whole pretzel. Makes 4 servings.

Nutrition Facts per serving: 188 calories, 9 g total fat, 27 mg cholesterol, 507 mg sodium, 20 g carbohydrate, 7 g sugar, 2 g fiber, 8 g protein.

 **Check This Out**   **Most strawberries have about 200 seeds.**

Piled high with layers of strawberries and pretzels, this pretty dessert is perfect for a princess.

CHOCOLATE MUD PIE

INGREDIENTS

Nonstick cooking spray

- $1/2$ cup all-purpose flour
- $1/4$ cup granulated sugar
- 1 tablespoon unsweetened cocoa powder
- 1 teaspoon baking powder
- $1/8$ teaspoon salt
- $1/4$ cup fat-free milk
- 1 tablespoon canola oil
- $1/2$ teaspoon vanilla
- $1/4$ cup chopped walnuts (if you like)
- 3 tablespoons packed brown sugar
- 2 tablespoons unsweetened cocoa powder
- $2/3$ cup water

Fresh raspberries (if you like)

Vanilla frozen yogurt (if you like)

UTENSILS

9-inch pie plate
measuring cups
measuring spoons
medium bowl
wooden spoon
small bowl

small spoon
1-cup microwave-safe glass measuring cup
hot pads
wire cooling rack
ice cream scoop (if you like)

1 Turn on the oven to 350°F. Lightly coat the pie plate with nonstick cooking spray. Save until Step 3.

2 Put the flour, granulated sugar, the 1 tablespoon cocoa powder, baking powder, and salt in the medium bowl. Stir with the wooden spoon to mix. Stir in the milk, oil, and vanilla. If you like, stir in the walnuts.

3 Pour batter into prepared pie plate. Put the brown sugar and the 2 tablespoons cocoa powder in the small bowl. Stir with the small spoon to mix. Put the water in the 1-cup glass measure. Put it in the microwave and cook on 100% power (high) about 1 minute or until bubbly. Use the hot pads to remove the glass measuring cup from the microwave. Carefully stir the water into the brown sugar mixture. Slowly pour brown sugar mixture over batter in pie plate.

4 Put the pie plate in the oven. Bake for 20 minutes. Turn off oven. Use the hot pads to remove the pie plate from the oven. Put pie plate on the wire rack. Cool for 20 minutes. Serve warm. If you like, serve with raspberries and scoops of frozen yogurt. Makes 6 servings.

Check This Out

Two-thirds of the world's walnuts are produced in California.

Nutrition Facts per serving: 127 calories, 3 g total fat, 0 mg cholesterol, 117 mg sodium, 25 g carbohydrate, 16 g sugar, 1 g fiber, 2 g protein.

INGREDIENTS

- **4 ounces purchased angel food cake (save the rest of the cake for another time)**
- **½ of an 8-ounce package reduced-fat cream cheese, softened**
- **2 tablespoons low-sugar strawberry preserves**
- **2 tablespoons fat-free milk**
- **3 cups fresh raspberries, blackberries, blueberries, cut up nectarines, and/or peeled and sliced kiwifruit**

1 Turn on the oven to 300°F. Put the cake on the cutting board. Use the serrated knife to cut the cake into cubes (you should have about 4 cups of cake cubes). Put cake cubes in the baking pan. Put the baking pan in the oven. Bake for 20 minutes. Turn off oven. Use the hot pads to remove the pan from the oven. Put pan on the wire rack. Stir 2 times with the wooden spoon. Let the cake cubes cool in the pan for 15 minutes.

2 Meanwhile, put cream cheese in the medium bowl. Beat with the electric mixer on medium speed for 30 seconds. Gradually beat in preserves and milk until smooth, stopping the mixer occasionally and scraping the sides with the rubber scraper.

3 Divide cake cubes among the dessert dishes. Top with fruit. Spoon cream cheese mixture over fruit and cake cubes. Makes 6 servings.

Nutrition Facts per serving: 140 calories, 5 g total fat, 14 mg cholesterol, 220 mg sodium, 21 g carbohydrate, 11 g sugar, 4 g fiber, 4 g protein.

UTENSILS

- **cutting board**
- **serrated knife**
- **measuring cups**
- **15×10×1-inch baking pan**
- **hot pads**
- **wire cooling rack**
- **wooden spoon**
- **medium mixing bowl**
- **electric mixer**
- **rubber scraper**
- **6 dessert dishes**
- **large spoon**

Get Mov!ng Strap on your bike helmet and go for a bike ride with your friends or your family!

You don't need pixie dust to make this light, fruity dessert, but your family may think you used a little fairy magic!

SEASONAL CELEBRATIONS

Hey, everyone! Surf's up! It's time to party! And Lilo and Stitch are along for the ride. After all, they love a good celebration.

And since celebrations change with the seasons, Lilo and Stitch have found recipes to help you party in the spring, summer, fall, and winter.

Now, we just need to keep Stitch out of trouble. On second thought, scratch that! Lilo and Stitch are here to party, and so are you! So have a blast and get cooking. Make your celebration one to remember!

And don't forget to tell Lilo and Stitch "mahalo!"

(That's "thank you" in Hawaiian.)

PARTY

DESIGN YOUR OWN
Fruit Pops

INGREDIENTS

- 3 cups fresh fruit such as cantaloupe cubes, strawberries, seedless grapes, star fruit slices (carambola), and/or kiwifruit chunks
- 1 6- to 8-ounce carton plain low-fat yogurt
- 1 tablespoon honey
- 1/8 teaspoon ground cinnamon

UTENSILS

measuring cups
cutting board
sharp knife
24 lollipop sticks
serving plate
measuring spoons
small bowl or glass
wooden spoon

1 If using strawberries, place them on the cutting board and use the sharp knife to cut off their green tops. Insert each lollipop stick into pieces of fruit. (You can put more than 1 piece of fruit on each stick.) Put all the fruit on serving plate. Save until Step 2.

2 For dip, put yogurt, honey, and cinnamon in the small bowl or glass. Stir with the wooden spoon to mix. Use as a dip for the fruit pops. Makes 6 servings.

Nutrition Facts per serving: 64 calories, 1 g total fat, 2 mg cholesterol, 25 mg sodium, 14 g carbohydrate, 13 g sugar, 1 g fiber, 2 g protein.

Food Facts

Honey is made by bees from flower nectar.

CHOOSE YOUR FAVORITE FRUITS TO MAKE YOUR OWN GALLERY OF DESIGNER POPS. IT'S A GREAT WAY TO WELCOME SPRING!

THESE FRUIT POPS ARE FABULOUS, DAHLING.

THEY ARE BOLD! DRAMATIC!

PARTY CUCUMBER SLICES

INGREDIENTS

- **1** cucumber
- **1** 6-ounce package refrigerated cooked chicken breast strips
- **$^1/_2$** cup fresh strawberries
- **$^1/_4$** cup light mayonnaise or salad dressing
- **$^1/_4$** teaspoon salt
- **$^1/_4$** teaspoon dried dillweed
- **$^1/_8$** teaspoon black pepper

UTENSILS

- cutting board
- sharp knife
- large bowl
- measuring cups
- measuring spoons
- wooden spoon
- small spoon
- tray
- plastic wrap

1. Place the cucumber on the cutting board. Use the sharp knife to slice off the ends. Holding the sharp knife at a slight angle, cut the cucumber into slices that are about $^1/_4$ inch thick. Save until Step 4.

2. Put the chicken on the cutting board. Use the sharp knife to chop the chicken into small pieces. Put the chicken in the large bowl. Put the strawberries on the cutting board and use the sharp knife to cut off their green tops. Chop the strawberries. Put the strawberries in the bowl with the chicken.

3. Add the mayonnaise, salt, dillweed, and pepper to the chicken and strawberries. Stir with the wooden spoon to mix.

4. Use the small spoon to put some of the chicken mixture on top of each cucumber slice. Arrange chicken-topped cucumber slices on the tray. Serve right away or cover with plastic wrap and chill in the refrigerator for up to 2 hours. Makes 20 to 24 slices (10 to 12 servings).

Nutrition Facts per serving: 43 calories, 2 g total fat, 14 mg cholesterol, 254 mg sodium, 3 g carbohydrate, 2 g sugar, 0 g fiber, 4 g protein.

Food Facts

Cool as a cucumber isn't just a catchy phrase. The inner temperature of a cucumber can be up to 20 degrees cooler than the outside air.

SERVE THESE SLICES OF CRUNCHY AND COOL CUCUMBERS FOR THE ULTIMATE SPRINGTIME PARTY.

OOOH . . . GARDEN GRUB!

MARKET FRESH

Fruit Cups

INGREDIENTS

1   4-serving-size package fat-free sugar-free reduced-calorie white chocolate- or cheesecake-flavored instant pudding mix

2   cups fat-free milk

3   cups assorted fresh fruit such as strawberry slices, blueberries, raspberries, and/or kiwifruit slices

6   tablespoons low-fat granola

6   slices star fruit (carambola) (if you like)

UTENSILS

six 8- to 9-ounce disposable clear plastic tumbler-style cups

tray or shallow baking pan

measuring cups

large bowl

wire whisk

small spoons

measuring spoons

plastic wrap

1   Arrange the cups on a tray or in a shallow baking pan. Save until Step 3.

2   Put the pudding mix and milk in the large bowl. Whisk about 2 minutes or until smooth and mixture starts to thicken. Let pudding stand for 5 minutes.

3   Divide half of the pudding among the plastic cups. Top with half of the fruit. Spoon the remaining half of the pudding over the fruit in the cups. Top with the remaining half of the fruit. Sprinkle with the granola. Cover with the plastic wrap. Chill in the refrigerator for 1 hour before serving. If you like, top each serving with a slice of star fruit. Makes 6 servings.

Nutrition Facts per serving: 259 calories, 10 g total fat, 230 mg cholesterol, 509 mg sodium, 25 g carbohydrate, 1 g sugar, 3 g fiber, 17 g protein.

Check This Out   **Wisconsin produces more milk than any other state.**

FRESH FRUIT IS A GREAT SUMMER TREAT. ADD GRANOLA AND PUDDING FOR A MAGICAL TASTE FROM A WHOLE NEW WORLD.

FREEZE IT! SHAVED ICE

INGREDIENTS

- 1 **cup peeled fresh peach slices or frozen unsweetened peach slices**
- 1 **cup fresh or frozen raspberries**
- 1 1/2 **cups warm water**
- 1/4 **cup orange juice**
- 1/4 **cup honey**

UTENSILS

- **measuring cups**
- **medium bowl (if using frozen fruit)**
- **blender**
- **sieve (if you like)**
- **large bowl (if you like)**
- **rubber scraper (if you like)**
- **2-quart square baking dish**
- **plastic wrap**
- **large spoon or ice cream scoop**
- **potato masher (if you like)**

1 If you are using frozen fruit, place it in the medium bowl with the warm water for 15 minutes, then drain. Put fruit, water, orange juice, and honey in the blender. Cover and blend until smooth. If you like, set the sieve over the large bowl and pour the fruit mixture into the sieve. Use the rubber scraper to press the pulpy mixture through the sieve until just the seeds remain; throw away the seeds.

2 Pour the mixture into the baking dish. Cover with plastic wrap and freeze until the mixture is firm (about 6 hours).

3 To serve, remove the baking dish from the freezer. Let the mixture stand at room temperature for 10 minutes before serving. Use the large spoon or ice cream scoop to serve the mixture. (Or, if you like, break up the mixture. Put in the large bowl. Mash with the potato masher until the mixture is slushy.) Makes 6 (1/2-cup) servings.

Watermelon Ice: Make as directed above, except replace the peaches and raspberries with 2 cups cubed seeded watermelon and decrease the honey to 3 tablespoons. You may want to press the mixture through the sieve to catch any small seeds.

Nutrition Facts per serving: 69 calories, 0 g total fat, 0 mg cholesterol, 2 mg sodium, 18 g carbohydrate, 16 g sugar, 2 g fiber, 1 g protein.

On a hot summer day, put on your swimsuit and run through a sprinkler!

IF YOUR FREEZING POWERS EVAPORATED WITH THE SUMMER HEAT, THIS FRUITY SHAVED ICE WILL HELP YOU CHILL OUT AND REPLENISH YOUR POWERS.
I KNOW, I KNOW. FREEZE.

PUMPKIN PATCH
Pancakes

INGREDIENTS

- **1** recipe Yogurt Cream (see recipe, below)
- **2** apples
- **1/2** cup all-purpose flour
- **1/2** cup white whole wheat flour
- **1** tablespoon packed brown sugar
- **1 1/2** teaspoons baking powder
- **1/2** teaspoon pumpkin pie spice
- **1/4** teaspoon salt
- **1** egg
- **1** cup fat-free milk
- **1/2** cup canned pumpkin
- **1** tablespoon canola oil

    Nonstick cooking spray

UTENSILS

- 2 small bowls
- measuring spoons
- spoon
- cutting board
- sharp knife
- measuring cups
- medium bowl
- wooden spoon
- whisk
- nonstick griddle or skillet
- rubber scraper
- pancake turner
- serving plate
- foil

1 Make the Yogurt Cream. Save until Step 8. Put the apples on the cutting board with stem sides up. Use the sharp knife to cut each apple into quarters. Cut the core out of each apple quarter and throw away the cores. Cut the apples into 1/2-inch sticks. Save until Step 6.

2 Put the all-purpose flour, white whole wheat flour, brown sugar, baking powder, pumpkin pie spice, and salt into the medium bowl. Stir with the wooden spoon to mix.

3 Crack the egg into a small bowl. Beat with the whisk until yolk and white are mixed. Add the milk, pumpkin, and oil to egg. Beat with the whisk until ingredients are well mixed.

4 Add egg mixture to flour mixture. Stir with a wooden spoon until dry ingredients are wet. (The batter should be somewhat lumpy, not smooth.)

5 Lightly coat a nonstick griddle or heavy skillet with nonstick cooking spray. Put the griddle or skillet on a burner. Turn heat to medium and let griddle or skillet get hot. (To check if the griddle or skillet is ready, carefully sprinkle a few drops of water on the surface. The water will dance across the surface when the griddle is hot enough.)

6 For each pancake, pour about 1/4 cup of the batter onto the hot griddle or skillet and use the rubber scraper to spread the batter to a 4-inch circle. Put one apple stick in the circle of batter so that the apple stick goes over the edge of the pancake to one side (this will be the pumpkin's stem). Cook over medium heat until pancakes have slightly bubbly surfaces and the edges are slightly dry (about 2 minutes).

7 Turn the pancakes over with the pancake turner. Cook until bottoms are golden brown (about 2 minutes more). Remove pancakes from the griddle or skillet and put on the serving plate. Cover with foil to keep warm. Repeat until all of the batter is used. Turn off burner. Remove griddle or skillet from the burner.

8 Serve warm pancakes with the Yogurt Cream and any leftover apple sticks. Makes 8 to 10 pancakes.

Yogurt Cream: Put one 6- to 8-ounce carton vanilla low-fat yogurt and 1/4 teaspoon pumpkin pie spice in a small bowl. Stir with spoon to mix. Makes about 2/3 cup.

Nutrition Facts per pancake and 1 tablespoon yogurt cream: 137 calories, 3 g total fat, 28 mg cholesterol, 156 mg sodium, 24 g carbohydrate, 10 g sugar, 2 g fiber, 6 g protein.

Pumpkins aren't just for jack-o'-lanterns! They are also good for eating. Celebrate the autumn harvest by adding pumpkin to your pancakes.

gooey, sticky CARAMEL SUNDAES

INGREDIENTS

- **2   medium red apples**
- **2   medium green apples**
- **1   tablespoon lemon juice**
- **¹/₂   cup caramel ice cream topping**
- **¹/₂   of an 8-ounce container frozen light whipped dessert topping, thawed**
- **1   cup low-fat granola or toasted corn and wheat cereal flakes with oats**

UTENSILS

cutting board
sharp knife
large bowl
measuring spoons
8 dessert dishes
spoon
measuring cups

1 Put the apples on the cutting board with stem sides up. Use the sharp knife to cut each apple into quarters. Cut core out of each apple quarter and throw away the cores. Chop the apples into small pieces. Put apples and lemon juice in large bowl and toss to mix.

2 Divide the apple mixture among the dessert dishes. Drizzle each with 1 tablespoon of the ice cream topping. Spoon whipped dessert topping onto each. Sprinkle each with 2 tablespoons of the cereal. Serve immediately. Makes 8 servings.

Nutrition Facts per serving: 180 calories, 3 g total fat, 0 mg cholesterol, 75 mg sodium, 38 g carbohydrate, 23 g sugar, 3 g fiber, 2 g protein.

Get Moving — When the leaves start to fall off the trees, rake a leaf pile and jump in!

EXPLORING, POUNCING, AND PLAYING AT THE WATER HOLE KEEP SIMBA AND NALA ACTIVE. REMEMBER TO KEEP ACTIVE TOO (BUT TRY NOT TO GET INTO A STICKY MESS).

DANGER? *HAH!* I WALK ON THE WILD SIDE. I LAUGH IN THE FACE OF DANGER! *HA HA HA HA!*

Snow-Topped PARTY CUPCAKES

INGREDIENTS

- 1   16.75-ounce package plain or confetti angel food cake mix
- 1   8-ounce container frozen light whipped dessert topping, thawed
- 3/4   cup flaked or shredded coconut

UTENSILS

- 2 muffin pans with twelve 2 1/2-inch cups
- 36 paper bake cups
- measuring cups
- very large mixing bowl
- electric mixer
- rubber scraper
- spoon
- hot pads
- wire cooling racks
- small spatula or table knife

1 Turn on the oven to 375°F. Line the muffin cups with paper bake cups. Using the mixing bowl, electric mixer, and rubber scraper, prepare the cake mix following the package directions. Spoon some of the batter into each muffin cup, filling each cup a little more than half full.*

2 Put muffin pans in oven. Bake about 12 minutes or until tops look dry and are brown. Use the hot pads to remove the muffin pans from the oven. Put the muffin pans on the wire racks and let cool for 10 minutes. Tip the muffin pans to carefully remove cupcakes onto the wire racks.

3 Line 12 more of the muffin cups with paper bake cups. Spoon some of the remaining batter into each muffin cup, filling each cup a little more than half full. Bake and cool as in Step 2. Turn off oven.

4 When cupcakes are completely cool, use the small spatula or table knife to spread the whipped topping over the tops of the cupcakes.** Sprinkle with coconut. Makes 36 cupcakes.

*Note: Cover and refrigerate the remaining batter while the first batch of cupcakes is baking.

**Note: You can frost as many cupcakes as you need and freeze any remaining unfrosted cupcakes. Put in a single layer in a freezer container. Cover and seal. Freeze for up to 1 month. Thaw and frost as desired. The amount of whipped topping and coconut given in the ingredient list is for 36 cupcakes.

Nutrition Facts per cupcake: 69 calories, 2 g total fat, 0 mg cholesterol, 92 mg sodium, 12 g carbohydrate, 7 g sugar, 0 g fiber, 1 g protein.

Check This Out

Each year more than 20,000,000,000 (that's 20 billion!) coconuts are produced.

WHY, IT'S LIKE A DREAM! A WONDERFUL DREAM COME TRUE!

If you're planning a royal ball, be sure to include these cupcakes! The coconut looks like freshly fallen snow, but you can enjoy these treats year-round.

be cool
peppermint parfaits

INGREDIENTS

1. **4-serving-size package fat-free sugar-free reduced-calorie chocolate-flavored instant pudding mix**

2. **cups fat-free milk**

$^1/_2$ **of an 8-ounce container frozen light whipped dessert topping, thawed**

$^1/_8$ **to $^1/_4$ teaspoon peppermint extract**

Green or red food coloring (if you like)

Green- or red-colored sugar and/or multicolored candy sprinkles (if you like)

UTENSILS

measuring cups
large bowl
wire whisk
measuring spoons
medium bowl
wooden spoon
6 small dessert dishes
spoons
plastic wrap

1 Put pudding mix and milk in the large bowl. Whisk about 2 minutes or until smooth and mixture starts to thicken. Save until Step 3.

2 Put dessert topping and peppermint extract in the medium bowl. Stir with the wooden spoon to mix. If you like, stir in enough food coloring to tint the mixture.

3 Divide pudding among the dessert dishes. Top pudding with the topping mixture. If you like, sprinkle with sugar and/or sprinkles. Cover with plastic wrap. Chill in the refrigerator for 2 hours before serving. Makes 6 servings.

Nutrition Facts per serving: 94 calories, 2 g total fat, 2 mg cholesterol, 254 mg sodium, 14 g carbohydrate, 7 g sugar, 0 g fiber, 3 g protein.

Check This Out

Peppermint is often used to give foods additional flavor, and it is also found in some shampoos and soaps.

CHILL OUT WITH A LITTLE PEPPERMINT ON A WINTER DAY. THESE TOO-COOL PARFAITS ARE SURE TO HAVE YOU SHAKING YOUR TAIL FEATHERS.

Get Moving Log

Use this physical activity log to keep track of all activities that get you moving. Remember, all kinds of activities count, like riding your bike, walking the dog, dancing, and playing sports. If you like, ask your parents to make copies of this page so you can keep track of how much physical activity you get every week! Try to meet the goal of 60 minutes every day. That's what kids like Dash need to stay fit and strong.

DAY OF THE WEEK	ACTIVITY	GOAL	ACTUAL/ ACHIEVED
SUNDAY		60 MINUTES	
MONDAY		60 MINUTES	
TUESDAY		60 MINUTES	
WEDNESDAY		60 MINUTES	
THURSDAY		60 MINUTES	
FRIDAY		60 MINUTES	
SATURDAY		60 MINUTES	
TOTAL		420 MINUTES	

If you had a total of at least 420 minutes or 7 hours for the week, way to go! Dash would be proud. If you had fewer than 420 minutes this week, try to log more minutes next week. Look for more fun activities you can do to get moving.

Fruits & Veggies Log

Because fruits and vegetables are packed with vitamins and minerals to keep you healthy and strong, it's no wonder grown-ups keep telling you to eat them. And the experts agree. They say to eat 5 to 9 servings of fruits and vegetables each day. Use this chart to keep track of how many servings you eat every day. Remember to try new fruits and veggies whenever you can. You never know if you'll like it until you try it. And don't forget, the darker the color of fruit or veggie, the better. The dark color means it has more vitamins and minerals in it. If you want to keep your log for more than a week, ask your parents to make copies for you.

DAY OF THE WEEK	FRUITS AND VEGGIES EATEN	NUMBER OF FRUITS	NUMBER OF VEGGIES
SUNDAY			
MONDAY			
TUESDAY			
WEDNESDAY			
THURSDAY			
FRIDAY			
SATURDAY			
TOTAL			

How did you do? If you ate at least 5 servings of fruits and veggies each day (that's 35 servings for the week), great job! If you ate fewer than 5 servings of fruits and veggies each day, work to get more next week. Keep trying new fruits and veggies. You might just find a new favorite!

My Favorite Recipes

Use this page to keep track of all the recipes you make from this book. Keep notes of which ones were your favorite so you will remember to go back and make them again and again!